Escape from the Third Dimensi

CW01662686

ESCAPE FROM THE THIRD DIMENSION

AGBE BEN EPOU

Contact: P.O. BOX 1136,
Spring Valley, New York 10977, U.S.A.

For information about special discounts for bulk purchases,
please contact Agbe Ben Epou at the
above address or the website below:

www.agbeepou.com

Library of Congress Control Number: 0000TXU0017615940101

ISBN: 9780985274214

CONTENTS

Acknowledgments.. i

Chapter 1: The Biggest Secret in the Universe 1

Chapter 2: Blinding Oneself in the System 14

Chapter 3: Enslaving the Light Self Through the Economic System 32

Chapter 4: Holistic Healing Through Food and Plant Medicine 62

Chapter 5: My Lingering Eternal Questions 76

Chapter 6: Ayahuasca Spiritual Healing 87

Chapter 7: Nearly Killing My Shaman 124

Chapter 8: Return to El Mundo Mágico 152

Chapter 9: Healing Old Wounds 172

Chapter 10: Stopping the World 183

Chapter 11: Don Peyote Spiritual Healing 225

Chapter 12: Forgiveness 255

Chapter 13: Finally Escaping from the Third Dimension 303

ACKNOWLEDGMENTS

I want to thank all those souls who have helped me here on my journey. My special thanks goes to Mother Earth, Mother Ayahuasca, my family, especially my brother Essevi, don Mescalito and the spirit of Iboga.

CHAPTER 1

THE BIGGEST SECRET IN THE UNIVERSE

Since the fall of civilization, mankind has been baffled by the Universe. Different cultures and people have sought to understand it through religion, science, and technology. Various belief systems have been erected and employed by the few to keep people fighting among themselves. As a result, the vast majority of human beings have become unaware of who they really are. As all of this happened, great civilizations have fallen and new ones have arisen. Some of the fallen ones, which have sunken under oceans, are now believed as merely myths and legends. Fortunately, through all of this, a small percentage of the human population is seeing through the lies, machinations, and the manipulations of days of old. More and more *minds* are increasingly understanding that just because you cannot prove or see something does not mean that it does not exist. They are understanding that Infinity or God really does exist and that it is not a belief system. It is a fact and cannot be argued or explained away by a false science or religion.

To me, the biggest achievement that is occurring in this third dimension is the intuitive awakening of who and what human beings really are. People are more aware that they are not their gender, science, culture, religion or the technology they possess in their countries. The need to escape is propelling them forward, and they are remembering that there aren't really any mysteries in the universe. They are understanding that the biggest mystery in the universe is not that there is no death; it is not that if you ask for salvation you will find it no matter what you have done; it is not the law of attraction, or the fact that you are supposed to reach higher and higher into Infinity with each life experience; it is not that reincarnation is real and that it is only a tool to have an experience; it is not that the world is far more technologically advanced than governments around the world would have us believe otherwise; or the fact that extraterrestrial beings really exist.

The biggest mystery in the universe is YOU! It always stares at you every morning when you look in the mirror in the bathroom. You see *It* whenever you stare at another human being. It has always been there—in the open, in front of you. It has been patient, for the most part—waiting for you to accept and take ownership of a basic universal truth—you are God. Not the son, daughter, or child of God—***literally*** a piece of God. By this, I do not mean a "superior" being. This cannot be because there is no superiority between anyone or thing in the entire UNIverse. Human beings are nothing and everything all at the same time. They are not even better, smarter or superior to rocks, trees or animals. Unfortunately, the vast majority of us is not aware of this because we have been manipulated to believe in the "superiority" of beings and things. There is only the illusion or the static perception of superiority. Thus for really dark souls, this is a fantastic reality. In actuality, only galactic manipulations, prejudices, and negativity hold us back from realizing our ultimate potential.

As the onion is peeled away, one remembers or is awakened to the universal fact that there are different levels and states of awareness. Some things exist in very tangible forms; while in the other extreme, other things exist in absolute intangible, weightless forms. In the former case, the energy has been condensed to an extreme, minute vibration state of existence. Let us consider an animal such as a dog. The dog's body is less tangible than the rock, but nevertheless its energy still exist in a solid movable state. If we continue this train of thought, we see that there are other forms of life that are even less tangible. We can consider water or H_2O. Water is fluid, formless, but nevertheless tangible because we can put it in a bucket or a glass and *feel* its *mass*. Finally, we come to gas. Gas is so light that it is weightless. Furthermore, there are some types of gas that one cannot see or smell, but exist.

As you can see, there is a range of existence to a being. Once you understand this, then you can began to make the correlation between your own physical body and your soul or Light Self. A human being's physical body is tangible. Its energy has been reduced to a low vibration state. As we *peel* the onion away, we are quickly aware that inside our physical brain is the "mind." The mind is far, far less tangible than the brain. In fact, it is safe to say that it is intangible. Consider how your thoughts come to you. Do they come to you in "hard" physical wave forms? No! They are light, effortless. Finally, we have the Ultimate Light Being behind the mind. This is the most intangible form that exists within each human being and animals. This is God, a piece of God. But, please don't forget the rocks, trees, and plants. They are also an intelligent being. Intelligent energy exists in different and various states of awareness. As Einstein said, Energy = M x C^2. It cannot be created or destroyed. It can only change form. When one considers this even without any spiritual experience, one can see that a human being who dies does not really die. The body decays (i.e., changes its state of being).

The soul then leaves the physically *dead* body usually almost immediately. The Light Being is greeted by its soul group—siblings, parents, grandparents and others who had long ago passed. After a life review with Infinity, another physical body is selected for another experience. Once the Light Being leaves the physical body, it is fully aware of all of its abilities. One could imagine the soul as a fluid, none physical circular beam of light, which is capable of taking *any* form it desires. It is capable of turning itself into a weapon or simply drawing out a weapon from within. Any source of weapon you can think of, it has the ability to manifest it. This is not science fiction. It is very real. The soul is so well-equipped that It fears nothing.

Let us consider what one of Dr. Brian Weiss's patients says about the nature of creation. On page 144 of Same Soul, Many Bodies, Patrick states, "My world is ancient and yours is very young, yet the difference is as nothing in the scope of time. Time is like a breath out and a breath in by a cosmic god. The out-breath is the creation of stars, planets, galaxies, and universes. The in-breath brings them all back into one incredibly small and dense point of dust in the god's lungs. The respiration of time, in and out, occurring in an endless number of cycles, hints at the nature of eternity."

From my current vantage point, it is intuitively clear that everything is literally imbued with the essence of Infinity. A piece of light form of Infinity, the none-solid, fluid part is literally imbued in physical matter, liquids, and gas. When one intuitively understands this, and the fact that the concepts of birth and death are merely a static state of perception, then one comes to an obvious conclusion: The soul is not really "created." It was only imbued within matter. There is no such thing as children, sons, or daughters of God. The physical body is not really physical. It can change from physical to none physical and vice versa. Everything is possible in the universe.

Unfortunately, most humans are sound-asleep spiritually. The spiritually unaware keep each other in line as slaves by frowning upon those who ask basic questions such as, "What is the soul," and "If God is all powerful, then why do we have so much chaos." Some people reach quick, incorrect conclusions. This would not annoy me if they even bother to research those conclusions or listen to the calm, peaceful voice within themselves.

Then there are those cynics, religious and none religious, who are so in denial that they absolutely refuse to even look and read about what is going on in the world. Even those who have some sense of the history of secrecy hide behind expressions like "It's just a conspiracy theory," or "I don't believe in conspiracy theories," and "If they were trying to rule the world, why haven't they after two thousand years?"

This later question is my absolute favorite because it depicts the depth of how really blind some beings are. To those people who make such absurd statements, I say to you, stop and consider why human beings use less than 10[1] percent of their brain. This is such a basic question that has been ignored for thousands and thousands of years. Some people are satisfied with a religious or a scientific answer, but for the love of God, how can this not be curious to you?

The interesting thing is that I have also heard some say that if one used more of one's brain capacity, one would become unbalanced and sick. Seriously, *sick*? The world has not been conquered and enslaved *yet*?

There is more than one type of slavery—one is with physical bars, and the other is without bars to make you think

---

[1] This is generous. It is probably about 3%, for 97% of our genes is considered junk DNA.

you're free. If humanity refuses to consider its ultimate Light Self, it will always be stuck in a denser version of energy—the mind. When you look at the world from that perspective, you will not be able to see the whole picture. You will not be able to use more of your mind. You will not be able to understand the nature of energy which is not physical. How can one understand that one's mind produces energy when one is only dimly aware of one's Light Self? It's extremely difficult. Maybe I should be less passionate, emotional about the current direction of the collective human *mind*, but it is extremely difficult when I know that the essence of anyone is me, my own ultimate Light Self.

Well, I suppose the good news is that at least *I* will be able to escape from the Third Dimension despite what my other soul mates do. I no longer doubt this because I remember being free once. Then *life* happened, and I became *a human being*. That was when the problems began. At that time, the concept of death and God were not a problem for me. That was a very long time ago. I did not worry about none existence. I simply existed, worry-free.

Like a lot of children, I loved playing with paper airplanes, kites, and so forth. Unlike most children in my village in Togo, I had a dear friend with whom I would play, sing, and sometimes dance.

I was a resilient child who never gave up on anything, especially when I was failing at something. I sought to know *what is* instead of what I was simply told. My best quality was my capacity to persevere despite setbacks and major challenges. It seems that when the going gets tough, I kept going.

As I write now, I understand that there are simple moments in our lives that remind us of who we are. An example of this is my banana story. A neighbor in our village had once promised me some bananas and said:

"Come back in an hour."

I ran around the village playing with my leaf airplane until the hour passed. I was at his door precisely fifteen minutes before the time expired. My eyes gazed upon his.

"I don't have them yet. Come back in a little while."

I began to wonder if he were lying. I thought about not going back, but something pushed me to find out. Less than an hour later, I was at his door waiting for my bananas. Still, there were none. Instead of running joyfully with my kite, I walked away disappointed. As I was leaving, he looked into my eyes—intently and understood my personality. It was a look as if to say: Doesn't this kid ever give up? At the time even I would not understand myself. Though I may falter, I always regain my balance.

I returned in the late afternoon, and he indeed had the bundle of bananas for me. I thanked him and departed joyfully.

The above ordinary story is important because it has reminded me time and time again of the importance of never giving up at critical points in my life.

Another important thing that I would take with me when I was nine or ten years old deals with two brothers. It was somewhat rectangular and its center was bare. I did not know exactly why I often found myself in the house, but I suppose it was because of two men who lived there. One of them, the younger brother, intrigued me very much. He appeared to be in his mid-forties. Presently, I stood by watching him swat at the empty air. He took a swing at something at his face, as if it were mortally menacing him beyond the visible world. Every once in a while he would sit down to relax only to get up again swatting his hands at the air, annoyed and afraid.

My eyes turned to the room to the left. There lied the body of a 15-year old tall boy whose image would remain with me for my entire life. His visage seemed neutral, undisturbed. Yet, to my mind, this boy whom I had known in our village was gone. In the past, I had stood at the window many times seeing other dead bodies from the side of the street pondering death—dwelling on death—thus beginning to create a belief system that this life was all there is.

My attention went back to the man. He had gone somewhere in the distance. Darkness fell upon the air and evening resided all around me. I decided to go home. The next day, the younger brother was dead! Four years later, his older brother would follow.

When I was ten years old, my indoctrination in various forms of worship began to solidify. They included science and education, culture, gender (i.e., being a man versus a woman), ethnicity (i.e., being Black, White, etc), and religion. I suppose it started with this latter element. I spent most of my earlier childhood with my paternal grandparents in a village in Togo, West Africa. Nearly everybody around me used the word "Mawu," which translates into English as "God." I considered the notion, not dismissing it or accepting it. I was objective. In school and church, our teachers and priests taught us that God created us. They mentioned something about the soul, but failed to explain how we exist. They wanted us to simply *believe* without much in depth explanation about the nature of the soul. In fact, most people around me, especially the adults would chastise me verbally or with a frown whenever I seem to depict a facial confusion or vocal disagreement. But, all I really wanted to know was how we exist—the different levels of the state of existence, on the physical to the most light. They claimed that God created us human beings. I asked how and was told that only God knows. This never made sense to me.

By the time I was thirteen years old, I lost my cool conscious state of objectivity. I secretly became obsessed with knowing who and what God is; and perhaps, the none-existence of God. By the age of seventeen when my younger brother died, I did not believe in God. Out of politeness and sometimes lingering curiosity, I went to church with friends, but only rarely. They made me kneel down like them to pray. My intuition told me that there was something off about this. The lingering question was always the same in my head:

If God is so great, then why do we bow down to him? Isn't He too great for that?

In my senior year in high school, one of my Caucasian friends frequently came to my house with his "elders" with the Book of Mormon. They were trying to convert me. I considered him to be a good person. He was polite and respectful, but he just was not answering my basic questions of existence. I posed questions after questions and became more and more confused with his contradictory answers. Eventually, he became tired of my questions and stopped coming to my house with his elders. Throughout the years, other religions would try to convert me, but only the most institutionalized would be successful—science.

I had escaped religion, and so I thought. Little did I know that I should have taken science more seriously—to study it objectively in order to have really escaped it. If I had done so, I would also have understood that life can be quite beautiful. I would also have understood much sooner that the universe can be quite painful when one is blind. Specifically, I would have perceived the fact that science is the most pernicious type of religion there is. It has very few tenets of truth. If I had challenged science within my own mind, I would have been able to ward off the inter-dimensional beings who were sent after me. More importantly, I would have escaped sooner, not only from the Third Dimension, but all slave-state dimensions.

Unfortunately, I was drawing in lies, manipulations and fear. It was so awful that I needed divine intervention. In 2007, when my mind was firmly locked in the physical vehicle, my deceased father came to warn me that I was going to "die beaucoup." At first, I was flabbergasted, awestruck, doubtful, for I had become unaware of the nature of existence. As a result, I had to fight dark entities night after night to stay alive. One night in bed, I had enough, and decided to face the music.

"I have to do this myself!" I said aloud with a frown, thinking about the entities that were attacking me. I was lying on the white carpeted floor without a bed frame. My body was to the right side. It was like turning around with the utmost determination to face an enemy after running away for so long. Once the decision is made, there is an impelling force that knows no fear, at least in those few minutes, and if the warrior should forget later, he or she will draw upon that moment when he faced the fear and stood his ground.

During the ensuing year and a half, I had visions, engaged in inter-dimensional combats, and received the ultimate universal message— that we are all literally a piece of God. Perhaps what was far more mind boggling is learning that every soul that advances increases the overall goal of Infinity. In this message, which was so lucid, and physically real, and far more sharp and colorful than the physical world, I beat my stepfather to death with a bat. Blood gushed from his body as he fell against the wall behind me. In that very instant, I was made to feel how what I had done would slow down the Universal Plan. Infinity screamed out with "no." There was no judgment. I understood without a shadow of a doubt that I was God, a piece of Infinity that needed no permission to exist. I had no master, no one to bow down to.

I understood that I had to take ownership of my every decision and thought. Then I remembered my childhood animal friend—the ram. I remembered his Infinity. I understood twenty years later that even animals, rocks, and plants are God. They were not created by a so-called superior creator. Creation, in the basic scientific and traditional sense of the word is an absolute manipulation, a lie! I became intuitively aware of the fact that the manipulation runs so deep that it goes beyond this physical, solid dimension. After the major message in May of 2009, I kept thinking about what Einstein said, "Energy cannot be created or destroyed." This immediately resonated with me as God cannot be created or destroyed.

Now I stare at people of different races and culture and think about the universal message: We're all connected. The Hasidic Jewish children that I saw at the public library last week are basically the same as me. The East African that I used to be friends with is me, and I am him, though our cultures and belief systems are different. There is the static perception of separation. We are all connected. *Every soul is important and cannot be tossed aside.* An image of Avon, my stepfather just came to mind. I recall the last time I saw him. He was shivering with fear as I spoke to him about murdering my younger brother.

There is a oneness. There is one consciousness. But at the same time there are many gods, for each individual Light within the mosaic whole represent a piece of the whole.

There is no sin: only negative and positive experiences.

With my awakening, I began to understand how the human population has been manipulated and controlled for thousands of years by its leaders and entities just beyond the visible world or dimension. Up to that point I was still afraid of death. However, a few months after my out of body experiences, death became something to look forward to: as long as I did not cheat. As a result, I started questioning everything—the whole societal system. I intuitively understood that all wars served a purpose. I was able to connect the dots within this physical dimension and the "next invisible" level of consciousness. The level of control includes the economic and business, political, nutritional, military, religious, science, intelligence, and education systems. Every element has been penetrated.

Over the ensuing months, my mind accepted my soul's message as visions after visions that I had came true year after year. I understood intuitively that I am immortal and that the traditional perception of death and birth are merely a static perception (i.e., a minute frozen caption) of the whole of Infinity. I began to revisit my former experiences to piece the puzzle together. One of the first things that came to mind was the "snake." I began hearing and seeing symbols of the snake everywhere. When I was in Kpalimé in 2009, I kept hearing the word used. I was told that the "snake" was with Togbui Sikpui in our house. If you did not read my first book, let me briefly explain what Togbui Sikpui is. It is a wooden chair in a small shed-like structure-housing. This small building, which "has" my ancestors' spirits had the snake with it. Naturally when I hear the word "snake," I think of the physical creature. Nevertheless, my intuition told me that this was more than a physical, biological being. My oldest aunt also clarified this for me.

"It is not an actual snake," she said, reading my thoughts.

"Then what is it? A spirit?"

"Yes, it's not physical."

"What is the snake doing there? How?"

My aunt was quiet. This indicated that she did not know the answer.

"Marco came to pray to it several times. He became blind."

"Why would he become blind?"

Marco was an older relative.

"The spirit caused him to be blind?"

"You can't ask it ill-will. It was during this time that I started thinking about how it could be that this being could exist beyond visible light.

Could it even exist? Yes!

To me, this was possible because I had had many experiences substantiating this before returning to the African continent that summer. I had nearly used the Light weapons within my body to chase away these beings. The snake therefore was a real possibility though I could not see it physically. It was also at this time that I put an end to my family's cultural tradition of animal offering to such beings. This was a major step toward my spiritual awakening, for it was an act of self-recognition. I recognized that I was a slave, and wanted to be free. To do this, I had to face the biggest demon there is: the mind. It nags: always annoying the interior Light with mundane questions.

CHAPTER 2

BLINDING ONESELF IN THE SYSTEM

When I was a child in Togo, West Africa, I was told that formal education is the key to having a successful future and access to knowledge. When I came to the United States of America, this foolish and insane idea was further hammered into my *mind*. I was even told that the more educated a person is, the more likely that person is to do well in life economically and financially. I bought into this lie. In fact, I was so indoctrinated that I studied like crazy, rarely making time for a relationship.

It was not until I started working on my first master's degree when the terrible and horrific truth started dawning on me consciously—the education and economic systems were destroying human beings' inner calm and peace. I began to understand that the two systems are highly linked together. I understood this consciously, but I was more or less clueless as to how these two systems served to hold us as slaves beyond the limited five senses. For the time being, I would only understand the negative effects that they produced for me as well as for other students.

I finished the university in four years with three degrees: a Bachelor of Science in Economics, a Bachelor of Science in Business Administration, and a Bachelor of Arts in French.

Still, I did not feel smarter. If anything, I did not learn a thing about who I really am beyond the visible five senses. My physics and biology courses focused only on the biological elements of who we are. Darwin and his criminal, ridiculous propaganda theories, which were presented in these universities as truth further blinded my spiritual awareness. Overtime, I was kept busy with this mostly false belief system—science. Religion did not get me, but science had a strangle-hold on me, mostly because it was an institutionalized daily ritual that lasted for four years.

At the end of the four years, I graduated with a 20-something thousand dollar debt. It was in 1999 and it was a good price, considering that I had attended a private university that initially cost $25,000 a year. I did not worry much about the debt because I was optimistic in those early years of life. I recalled walking with one of my female dorm mates. We were walking past the financial aid office when we began talking about the amount of debt we would be accumulating at the end of our four years. She had a sad look on her face.

"Listen, the good thing about these loans is that I don't have to pay if I die," I said with a smile.

"But you'll be dead Kossi," she said, laughing boisterously.

In hindsight, I did not worry about debt or death in those days. The fear of death did not kick in until my junior year when I started taking a philosophy course.

In addition to the debt, there is also an unheard of pressure. The amount of pressure that students face in college and in particular Ivy League schools is tremendous. I have seen major effects of this when I worked the overnight shift at Columbia University. My job consisted of answering and resolving housing issues. The problems were various. They consisted of students being locked out of their dorms, not having power in their rooms to medical responses. As you can see Reader, some of these issues required me to go to students' dorms. I responded to attempted suicides and actual suicides with and without my manager. Once, a student threw herself out of a shaft and landed in the basement concrete floor. My manager prevented me from seeing the actual body. However, later after the female student was taken to the hospital where she later died, my manager and I returned to the scene where I saw some of the blood on the floor. I quickly turned my head for I was not a big fan of blood. You see Reader, we usually log all incidents that took us out of the office. However, incidents like these were kept out of the official logs. The overnight manager reports them directly to his boss and the director. In hindsight, I see what they were doing. The logs were accessible to nearly everyone in the housing department. Evening employees had to hide some of their problems just in case they became a legal issue or if they got out of hands.

At another point, one of our own student employees threw himself off the roof because of too much pressure. I actually knew him fairly well. We had many interesting global discussions about religions and general problems in the world. He even came to the Bronx to visit me once. He seemed relatively happy. I was aware of the fact that he was not doing well in some of his courses, but I knew that he was extremely bright, probably brighter than I am. So, it was a surprise to learn that he had committed suicide. It turned out that he was failing most of his courses and his father was putting pressure on him.

This brings me to an overall important point: the worship of the intellect is taking a toll on our young people. They are committing suicide in universities, especially Ivy League

I started to ask myself: *What am I to them? A slave?* Yes, I was and I myself had accepted it; for there were days when I slept only for an hour before returning to work.

Antoinette not only expected her teachers to be extremely dedicated to the job preparation-wise, but also in terms of classroom management. She expected her staff to inform her about every disruptive student in their classes. The foreign language teachers were told to write referral forms on all students who disrupt the learning process. It was not acceptable for us to ignore or overlook things such as cursing, loud noise, constant chatting, or students putting their heads down on the desk. All students who violate the rules were to be spoken to and then written up if the behavior continued. The discipline form that we filled out was to be given to her, and not to the assistant principal at the Student Management Office. This unwritten hierarchical structure served two functions. First, it allowed Antoinette to remain abreast of what was transpiring with her teachers and maintain control. Second, it provided us teachers support. Although I found this to be helpful, there were still major behavioral problems in the classes.

I recalled the first couple of weeks with distaste. My worse course was the eighth period. I remember once walking into class about two minutes before the bell rang. One of the students near the right of the door was banging a half-frozen water bottle on the desk and talking. This was as bad if not worse than New York City. There were constant boisterous shouting. The words "f—k you" and "f—kn this" were common place. To contain such negative energy and to get some learning out of them, I gave daily quizzes. At times I even gave two quizzes: one at the beginning and one at the end of the class. Honestly, I expected the students to be much better behaved because we were in the "suburbs." That was just a silly expectation because at times it felt like New York City was better.

I was constantly on the phone with parents. I also had parent-teacher conferences, which Antoinette always attended. I can say with every ounce of purity within my body that I did the very best that I could. By the end of the first semester, the students began to behave. However, one of the students would test my resolve. During the seventh period class, while I began testing, Ancha, a seventeen year-old female, decided to sleep with her head down on the desk. It was the beginning of the class and the rest of the students were behaving well. The school, like all schools that I know of, does not allow students to put their heads down on their desk in a sleeping position. She was sitting in the center of the room and I asked her to raise her head. She refused. I asked her again but it was to no avail. I went out the door and asked the security guard to take her out of the class. Once the guard showed up, Ancha got up and left the class on her own volition.

I had repeatedly told the students that they had to go to the nurse's office if they were not feeling well. In this case, she did not seem to be ill.

When the seventh period ended, I started the last class. I did not remember why the classroom door was locked, but I suppose I should have left it like that. In any case, there was a knock on the door. I looked through the glass opening in the center; Ancha stared at me with a smile. She said she had left a notebook or something like that in the room and wanted to retrieve it. I hesitated for a second, and then went against my better judgment, I opened the door for her and headed toward the front of the room to resume my teaching. Suddenly now, I felt a strike upon my head. I put my hand to the spot to ease the pain. The lock with which she had hit me was on the ground, broken. I took one step toward her, and gave her a piercing look as if to say: *You must be kidding, right?* I held my gaze as if trying to communicate with her psychically. *I am bigger and stronger than you.*

The lock did not suffice, for quickly now, she went for the student desk. She held the desk in her hands and I stared at her as if she were crazy. She was determined to throw the desk at me as best as she could. The students moved back in fear. By now, the class had gotten completely out of control and it seemed that the proximate hallways knew about the chaos. Ancha left the class. Antoinette, the security guards, and the school police officer all showed up.

Some of the students were laughing at me.

"I would not have left her hit me," one girl near the door said vehemently. Quite a few of the students were also laughing and ridiculing me.

Later, either the second or the third day, Antoinette took me to the principal's office for a meeting. I described to the principal what happened with Ancha.

"This does not make sense. Why would you hit someone after they bought you a cake…what was the cake for?"

"It was her birthday," I answered.

"Agbe cooks for them…to bribe them," Antoinette said with a knowing smile.

"That's got to stop. No more cooking the children," she said sternly.

"Alright," I said.

Because I do not recall what the principal's exact words were here, I will explain what I learned next.

She said that Ancha was seeing a psychologist for personal issues. Her father was battling cancer. Her mother was either in her native country or somewhere else.

"She said she was praying in the bathroom asking God to forgive you," Beverlyn said.

"It would have been nice to have known this earlier," I said.

Several months later, Ancha was let back into the school again. My chairperson found herself in the bathroom with her. One of my AP French female students who witnessed the incident came to me laughing. According to her, Ancha had asked sarcastically why she was following her and if she "wanted her to eat her pussy." She made some threats to Antoinette. Ancha was expelled within days.

Some of the teachers took notice of this.

"They expelled her for insulting an administrator, but not when she assaulted a teacher."

I did not say anything. Instead, I tried to compose myself, to conceal my imminent laughter.

In June 2007, I received my end of year evaluation. All four categories were satisfactory except one. Antoinette asked to talk to me in one of the math rooms, which was directly across the Foreign Language and ESL Office. She sat to my right and began directly.

"Do you plan on staying in this profession?"

"Ah, yeah," I answered with my eyebrows raised.

"The presentation you gave," she said, "They didn't like it."

She was referring to a speech I had given in front of some of the faculty members and administrators about halfway through the academic year. She was right. It was a terrible presentation. My mind was all over the place and my words were incoherent. Only if she knew how right she was. I wanted *to stop* her. She was staring at me, waiting for her desired effect. I wanted to stop her, but was too shaken up by her insult. I was dead quiet. My eyes turned away from her gaze.

"In this profession, we are orators. We talk in front of people."

Another dead on statement! She was so accurate in everything she was saying, yet she herself could not understand the deeper cause. Neither could I. It was the way in which she proffered her statements that brought me great dismay. She was being tough, and I was being even "tougher" unconsciously without knowing it.

"There is something off about the way you speak, put your thoughts together."

"Has your family ever told you that?"

"No," I said with confidence.

Though I did not say anything to her, I did not appreciate the insult. I knew that she was bullying me, but I didn't know how *to stop* her. That is, I failed to her trap of actually considering the very idiotic idea that there was something wrong with my brain and the way I speak. When I started considering whether or not she was right, I was identifying or telling myself that there was a possibility that she might have been right. Thus, I let my mind torment me.

During the summer of 2007, early July, I learned that my Advanced Placement French students had done quite well on the nation-wide exam, better than the previous AP teachers—according to one of the assistant principals. Though this did not do away with the insult, I would remember how well they did for the ensuing years as I worked even harder.

During the ensuing academic school year, I found myself in the office alone one day working after hours on my lesson when I realized that there was indeed something off about the way "my" mind worked. I was sitting in front of the computer to the left creating my lessons for the next day. I rose from my sitting position to get something when I felt "it." I heard an echo in my mind from above. "What?" I said. This "*what*" resonated on top of my head as if it were coming from above the top of the ceiling, the top of my head. Many times after that I would feel this weird sensation.

Perchance Antoinette was right.

Yet, I did not feel that this was really me—the echo of thoughts. Immediately, I noticed myself perceiving what I said inside my mind. It was me, but not me. It was strange. I felt a distance between the two voices. I could hear every word being uttered inside my head as if someone else were saying them. I got up, walked to the center of the room near my chairperson's desk and stood still pondering all this. I was calmly trying to understand how this could be.

Why am I hearing every word I am saying loudly in my head?

This was most strange. Instead of exploring this like a serious truth seeker, I let it go.

The 2008-2009 academic year passed by with an array of personal and work problems and drama. My deceased father came to warn me that my death was imminent. I was chased and pursued by extraterrestrials who are currently controlling the planet. I was now working two jobs and doing my master's degree in education administration. I was overwhelmed with my bill payments. I wondered for whom in the world I was working so hard. Nearly all of my disposable income went toward bills, loans, and my mortgage payment. I realized that I made a huge mistake purchasing my house. I was working hard without ever seeing the fruit of my labor. My mortgage and utility bills were killing me. I spoke to a few friends. They encouraged me to keep the house because "it is an investment." I protested, saying that my health was taking a toll. I tried to explain that there was something fundamentally wrong with the system. They did not buy my explanation, so I stopped talking for the most part unless I met someone who was more sensible.

In terms of my job, I continued working hard like a madman. Like the previous year, I had four different preparations. Part of the problem was that Antoinette expected us foreign language teachers to create our own worksheets from scratch.

In June of 2009, things would take a turn for the worse at work. It began when my boss saw one of my male colleagues talking to me about his end of year evaluation that she had given him. We were near the office. He had a book metal cart with wheels with his belongings on it. Out of nowhere came our chairperson Antoinette. She was coming toward us from the west. Quickly now, and with a knowing smile on her face, she advanced toward us. With an incredible speed now, my colleague turned the evaluation letter upside down, and thus knocking over his books on the cart. The books and the other papers covered the evaluation. She posed us a question or two about what we were up to with a formidable look of deceit and revenge, and then she departed. I knew right then and there that she would retaliate for the mere fact that I had associated with a colleague she did not like.

Sure enough I was right. About two weeks before school ended, Antoinette, the other French teacher and I sat down to discuss our teaching assignments and strategies for the ensuing year. Antoinette had given me six preparations for the next year. Those of you Readers who are teachers may be wondering how this may be possible given that we can only teach five courses a day at the secondary school level. Well what Antoinette did was to combine the Advanced French 4 and 5 classes, which made it six to prepare for each day.

"That's too much," I said to her. She stared at me vaguely and did not say anything.

...Interruption!

I just went to the bathroom. As I entered, spider webs seized my face especially my nose area. For a moment, I thought it might have been real spider webs. Since I was not sure, I did not wipe it off my face. Instead, I looked in the mirror to examine it. I didn't see anything, so I returned to my writing. A few minutes later, it all disappeared except from my nose.

As I was saying, every year since I started working at the school district, I have been given four to six preparations. The administrators counted on me "having a job" as a form of silence. That is, because most people are afraid of losing their jobs, they either suffer the injustice or fight the small battles. Furthermore, the administrator counts on your fear of getting a bad classroom observation from speaking up. The principal, chairperson, or assistant principal will invoke words such as "differentiated instruction" to justify their deceit. This concept to a small extent is doable. However, for the most part it is a load of bull-shit. Teachers socially promote students while administrators, even the calm smiley ones lie, lie, and lie to keep their jobs.

Before the end of June 2009, I spoke to Kathy about reducing the number of teaching preparations. She never got back to me. I went to visit my relatives in Togo during the summer and returned two weeks before school started.

Upon returning, I went in person to see Kathy about the overload in my duty preparations. What she said next, to me, was an indication of her toughness as well as her dark stubbornness.

"Let's wait to see what Antoinette thinks."

I was baffled. My eyes rose and stayed immobile in suspension for what appeared as an eternity. Gingerly now, I overcame my surprise.

"When classes begin?" I asked softly with wide, astonishing eyes.

She answered yes with infinite calm.

It was the assistant principal's job to make the final decision about teachers' schedules. If one could rectify the schedule, it was definitely her. Yet, she wanted to speak to her subordinate first—despite the fact that I told her that I had already discussed the issue with my chairperson. I even suggested the split option between the two high schools as a possible solution, but my request went on death ears; and would remain so until about a week before the ensuing academic school year.

I walked away with a flabbergasted countenance.

"*She intends to fix nothing,*" I said to myself, stunned.

CHAPTER 3

ENSLAVING THE LIGHT SELF THROUGH THE ECONOMIC SYSTEM

To escape from slavery, one must first know that one is indeed a slave. This is especially difficult when the slave-state is a prison without bars. Because of the way the system is set up, the vast majority of people do not even know at the conscious level that they are prisoners. As a result, they defend the system.

I recalled one of my international economics professors defending the economic system with excitement. He said something to the effect of "thinking twice before holding up banners" to protest the World Bank economic decisions. I objected with, "But it's not working." We were discussing the effects of the World Bank and the IMF lending practices in regions such as East Asia and Africa. Do not get me wrong, some of the finest souls that I have met on my journey here on Earth have been teachers and professors. I myself am a foreign language teacher. However, I see that even they are caught in the web of the "mind," the worship of the intellect—a false religion which they will probably defend to the extreme, maybe because they have been inculcated for so long, or perhaps because their livelihood depends on it.

For six good years I too defended the system to students. I told them that they needed to study this or that to be successful in life. However, by the grace of Infinity such blind practice has ceased. After my spiritual awakening, I could no longer sleep at night knowing that I was propagating lies. Deep inside, I see now that I too was afraid of not having a job if I did the right thing. As I write now, I only have a few thousand dollars in my bank account. I am not rich or even remotely close to it. This is precisely the point—when is enough *enough*? When do we rise against this ludicrous, false religion manifesting itself through the education and economic systems as truth?

Most people go through their lives chained down as slaves mostly without being conscious of it. Only when the pain is most unbearable do they cast away the fears and rise like tranquil warriors. For me, my battle against the economic system commenced when I bought a house, and was officially hooked in the control system. I was working two jobs and everything was going well. I was a hard worker and did not think that there was anything wrong with working so much. After all, I had two tenants occupying two floors, and I was beginning to save money. The house had three floors. However, this would not last. Within a few months, both tenants lost their jobs and left. This was not what I wanted, but I had planned for the worse. I was still able to pay my mortgage and maintain my good credit. This worked for about two and half years. Then one day, I found myself in a hotel. The pipes on the third floor were broken, rendering the house completely inhabitable. I fixed them with the help of my insurance company.

While leaving the hotel to return to the house two days later, I stopped at a Tarot card reading place at the shopping center. It was then that I discovered that my health problems were due to being possessed by a lower dimensional entity for "eight" years. The psychic exorcised it out of my body and I returned to the house. A few days after returning home, I had further flooding on the second and third floors. Soon after that, other problems would ensue. A couple of the neighbors started complaining that there was sewage polluted water on their properties and it was coming from my house as well as two other houses. Apparently, the pipes under the ground that were connected to these other houses were broken. After doing much research, we the property owners learned that the problem arose because the pipes were old and were rotting. I could pay my mortgage, and even the broken pipes in the house, but to pay to repair the pipes underneath the ground was impossible.

The three of us went to the Mayor's Office to get help. We were told that they would do what they could. The repair estimate was about $60-70 thousand dollars. My mouth dropped. We had inherited a problem by virtue of having our houses on the property. When a house is inspected, such problems are usually not detected. One of the owners turned to me:

"I have already paid off the house…"

His facial expression depicted sadness. The other owner, whose house was to the left of mine shook his head.

"I am on fixed income."

He retired a long time ago.

"There is no way I am going to be able to pay for this. I won't! The problem was there before I got there," I said.

"It doesn't matter," the old white man said quickly, "It's under your name."

"I don't care."

"Then the bank will take it from you and you'll have bad credit."

"Bad credit? Please!" I said with a smirk, "I've lost so much money on the house. I've paid forty thousand dollars a year for the past three years, not to forget the down payment and the title fees." I was standing by his house now. The old man smiled.

"The last guy just left it."

"You mean the second to the last owner?"

"Yes."

"He just abandoned it?"

"He couldn't handle it anymore. The bank took it."

"Well," I said with a gingerly movement of the head, "It looks like the bank will have to take it again."

I left him and went to the front gate of the house. I stood there for the first time thinking about the economic system from a different perspective.

I'm literally part of Infinity and I have to keep doing this? Nonsense!

A few months after returning from Togo in 2009, I would drive to the house. I would stand in front of it, observe it and smile.

This is not my house. It has never been my house. It had always belonged to the bank!

My mind shifted to the Infinity message that I had several months thither: *I'm Infinity*. Why should someone who is literally a piece of God be working to survive? It did not make any sense to me anymore. It was that very same day that I was able to piece together my spiritual experiences and the enslaved physical world.

What is money?

I was on the veranda facing the backyard on the third floor of my house in the early months of 2009 when Lisa, the psychic who had been "helping" me called.

"How are you doing sweety?"

"I'm drowning in debt: the house, the pipes. This is an impossibility. I can't do it."

"It'll take you about five years to get things on track. You need to work out a monthly payment plan—"

"I won't do it!" I proclaimed with a frown.

I am not a slave.

"You can't imagine the incredible job opportunities that you're gonna get," she said in amazement, "Why?"

I did not care to ask her what in the world she was talking about nor did I really know why I uttered what I said next.

"That's the way it is supposed to be. We're supposed to help each other."

As I hung up the phone, I had a thought: *You're trying to squeeze as much money out of me because of the monetary gains that you see in my future.* I stood over the ledge of the house, enjoying the cool spring air. I was extremely calm inside. Thoughts of the global economic system came to me.

Gangsters! These banks are gangsters. Economic gangsters! I can't believe I voted for Barack Obama...Money is printed out of thin air and he bailed out Wall Street because 'They are too big to fail.' Why didn't I see it before?

I moved to the right side of the ledge.

This is a great view. I can see the top of everybody's house.

I smiled. *Barack Obama is a famous gangster. Ha, ha!*

I was laughing at myself. I signed a piece of paper in 2006. This piece of paper was money, and if I could or refuse to make payments, then the bank could take the house and I would lose my deposit. Thirty-five thousand dollars—gone! Eight thousand dollars to fix the third floor in 2007—gone! Forty thousand dollars a year for three years—gone!

Think Agbessi! You have a master's in economics. Stop being blind! The fractional reserve system!

A feeling of eureka overcame me with utter clarity. Banks are really gangsters. The fractional reserve system allows banks to loan more money than they actually have. It's brilliant.

Ha, ha! The economic system! Debt is slavery. No! I will not pay a single dollar more toward my mortgage!

I opened the third floor door and entered. I looked at the pipes that were fixed in the house. Then, I went to the bathroom. *The heater in here is still not completely fixed.* Then I walked out and looked up from the top of the stairs, I saw the third floor bathtub exposed.

This might cost a thousand dollars or two to fix.

I walked to the back yard exit. I opened the door to the second floor.

"Dude!" I smiled, "This is a fantastic gift!" I said out aloud, my thoughts changing.

"This is a gift disguised as a nightmare."

My smile became infinitely larger. My insurance company spent over twenty thousand dollars fixing the third floor alone, and they are not even done with the floor yet.

I looked up at the tiles. I walked to the kitchen. The floor, refrigerator, the walls, the windows—they were all f—ed up!

Fantastic! Quel cadeau! Ha, ha!

The tenants and the flood had deliciously destroyed the second floor. It would cost thousands and thousands of dollars to fix it. I opened the door to the entrance between the second and third floors. I looked at the formerly white walls. They had cracks in them. I closed the door and went to the first floor. It was in the same condition. The water tank had stopped leaking. This floor would also cost a fortune to repair. Brian, the insurance claim representative e-mailed me about a repair check he sent me a week or so ago. I told him that the money would not be enough to fix the house. He referred me to one of their repair people. I briefly considered fixing the house as much as I could, but other delicious thoughts were crossing my mind. In hindsight, Lisa who was a financial leech, was not completely useless. She called me one evening to ask for money to heal me spiritually.

"Your father is supposed to have a conversation with you soon."

A conversation with me?

"The guy who's supposed to do the job won't finish it. Why are you trying to fix the house? It's cursed…"

I hung up the phone, and images of a verbal argument flashed before my mind. I was with a being in Light form directly above my bed in an erect position passionately arguing. Later, I would understand that I was separated from my physical body. I cannot entirely remember what in the world we were verbally fighting about, but I stood my ground on moral basis. I was a hard wall that could not be moved no matter what the other being said.

The interesting thing was that the person doing the observation was my mind. My mind was trying to understand what was going on, but It was too confused. Later, I would understand that the mind can "become" an independent *being*, though not as advanced as the Ultimate Light Self. My mind was astonished to witness its Lighter Self arguing with another Light Being in a language that was out of this world—a language that I have searched for on the this planet, but have not heard since. I was so fluent in it—speaking it like what seemed a thousand miles an hour.

"Who is this guy?" my mind dimly asked.

After considering my out of body experience and Lisa's statements about my father, I came to the conclusion that she was right—that it was indeed my father who came to tell me about not fixing the house.

My decision made, I went downstairs to the first floor to pack my belongings. I took out my clothes and white jacket from the closest. I first cleared my huge pediatric foam mattress and placed a clean sheet over it. I put the sheet on the bed. As I stood there ironing my clothes, selective memories of the past came to me with calm. First, I recalled the fact that this was the place where my stomach problems began. My thoughts kept centering on a particular evening when I held my stomach, for the pain was unbearable. At first, I thought it was something that I ate. Then, I thought that it might have been the negative energy around me that I was feeling. Then, I posed myself a question: How can something outside your body able to affect your stomach so sharply? It did not make any sense, but I could not figure out the answer, so I let it go, and played some music as I packed.

A second memory came to me in waves of sounds and images as I listened to the music. I saw myself giving a friend a "massage." I do not remember the type of lotion I was using, but I was quite meticulous and supple. I thought about the *next level*, and I advanced *forward* a little, thinking about whether or not to cross the threshold.

"A part of me" deeply wanted to, and the physical manifestation in my body was now palpable. Touch after touch of the hand increased the need in my shorts and the surge of incomprehensible feeling in my chest area. My analytical senses were slowly being overwhelmed.

"Oh, it feels so good," she said in a moaning tone.

"Why is this need so great," I asked myself momentarily. It felt as if I had sex with her, we would have had to be at it for hours and hours for the need to have been appeased. I could not understand this intense urge, so I stopped to observe the emptiness.

"That's it," I heard myself say to her.

She was quiet and probably disappointed. I went to the living room, while she remained in the bedroom for a little while.

The last thing that I would recall quite often as I packed my things was what Dr. Brian Weiss said about souls. It does not matter where one comes from in the universe, when one is in human form, one experiences the same emotions such as anger, joy, depression and happiness the same way as any human being.

A week and a half passed and I was still in the house. The exquisite delicious thoughts that I had about *dropping* my house came back to me as I held a foreclosure letter in my hand. The bank gave me a month or so to make the payment before they file papers against me.

Market value!

I had it! The market value of the house was unprofessionally estimated to be about $150,000. Recall that I bought the house for $454,000. Applying what I had learned in my economic classes, a thought came to me.

The bank can only recover the current market value of the house.

I was sure the house was worth a lot less than $150,000 because of the underground piping issue. Assuming that it costs the two banks $30,000 to fix the pipes, this would lower their profit from $150,000 to $120,000. In addition, I thought that a professional inspector would not value the house even for $100,000, for it would cost tens of thousands of dollars to repair the interior. This did not even take into consideration the water that seeped to the base of the house. In addition, I would have another gift a few months later. Someone would break into the first floor to squat.

The first floor windows were broken. I smiled as I looked at the check that the insurance guy sent me. This was more good news. It had my name as well as the initial mortgage bank's name on it. The initial mortgage bank was no longer my bank. I tried to contact the *banksters*, but was unsuccessful. At that point, I was ecstatic because I knew I could not cash the check. There was no way I was going to run around town trying to get the original bank's signature on the check. The original loan was sold twice and I was making payments to the servicing companies. My insurance company insisted that they would only write the check to the initial mortgage company because that was what was on file. They said they had no obligation to anyone else.

In the meantime, I had to concern myself with finding a place to live before my plane left for Togo in mid-July of 2009. At that point, I still had good credit, but it was only a matter of time before the three credit bureaus updated my credit account for the worse. I quickly found a place about half an hour away. The renter ran my credit and it was still good. If the lady had bothered to run it again a month later, she would have realized that my credit score was now 588. She found me a one-bedroom apartment for $1,400, but I turned it down, for it was a little small for that price. Now, I was in a jam. I had bad credit and did not have a place to live. Somehow, I was not worried. Something calmed me down. It was a vision that I had a few weeks prior. It occurred during the sleep state one evening. I was close to my job, at the high school. I was driving my little car into a parking lot of the apartment complex. I did not know the address, but it did not matter, for I retained the visual of the place. Then, I was in another place. It seemed like two separate visions. In the other part of the vision, which was so, so vivid and physical, I found the place where I would live for the ensuing few years. I recall walking on the greenest grass that I had ever seen.

There were groups or sections of apartments in the complex. The trees seemed so soothing. Every step that I took on the grass felt sensuous. I felt my movements—so physical. However, it was a less dense sensation. I was with two of my Dominican friends. I had invited them to the apartment, probably to have dinner. I recalled walking in the living room, then I woke up. It would only be about five months later when I would understand the sensuous nature of the things I felt in this particular vision and others, including my lucid dreams. I would understand that the soul thinks that everything is beautiful: well, almost everything.

Given that I was fairly certain that there was something to this vision, I decided to pay heed to it. In late June, I drove around my job area. I went from location to location until I found the first place in the first part of my vision. I compared how I felt in the dream to the feeling I was getting at the first apartment complex.

Yes, this is the place!

However, I also knew that this would not be the place I would live. I left and called Harry, my realty person. I had hired him to help me find an apartment to rent. We went to several places. One of them was a few blocks from the house. The price was decent: $1,250 a month. Harry and I tried and tried, but I felt something was blocking our access. I thought about my brother and my father as perhaps being involved in this. The other place refused because I had bad credit. I explained the situation to the owner, but he had more faith in the credit system than he had in my personal promise.

As Harry continued the search for me, I also continued my own. I got one good laugh out of it. I found an apartment about fifteen minutes away from my house. This time, I explained my situation to the apartment owner ahead of time. He was alright with my circumstances. He was not there when I arrived. The maintenance man led me to the apartment. The floor was covered with grey tiles. They were old and unattractive.

"*Time is ticking!*" my mind reminded me. I decided to overlook the old unattractive carpet.

"How's the fridge?" I asked, walking toward the kitchen.

"It's alright," the tall, black maintenance man answered.

I suppose the question was unnecessary, for about thirty seconds later I had my real answer.

"Naw! Get out of here!" I said in astonishment.

He stared at me in surprise.

"Dude, do you *see* that!" I exclaimed, "They're still alive."

I took my eyes momentarily away from the fridge to look at the maintenance guy.

"How do you suppose these big roaches survive in this cold refrigerator?"

He offered me a sympathetic look as an answer.

"Well, let me go check out my other appointments. Thank you for showing me the place."

I walked down the stairs as fast as I could, hoping, wishfully hoping to escape on time. Somehow I was dreading meeting the owner at the entrance or outside the building. Quickly now, I picked up the pace. As I reached the door, a tall white guy greeted me with a smile with a slight European accent, though I could not identify the country.

"Did you see the apartment?"

"Yeah, I have some other appointments now. I am running a little late. I'll definitely call you."

"Alright."

I walked out of there with relief. When I got to the car, I called my mother to relate the story.

"It had roaches! And they were big. It reminded me of the Bronx. I don't ever want to cohabitate with cockroaches again. Non merci! Ojala que no!"

"Then you can't take it, but you're running out of time…"

About a week later, I found the place in my vision. As soon as I arrived and caught a glimpse of the trees, I knew right away that it was the one. The location of the trees matched my visual recollection in the dream. The apartment owner was very understanding of my situation. Besides, I was prepared. I came with copies of my pay stubs. I signed the lease two or three days later—leaving me with just enough time to move my belongings into the two bedroom apartment. Because I had trusted my instincts, which was just really my inner Light talking to my mind, things worked out. Nevertheless, I was a little concerned about my financial situation. If I recall correctly, I had about twenty dollars left in my bank account. I took the rest to Togo for food and expenses. During this trying financial time, I asked myself why I had gotten myself in so much debt. It was because I too had bought into the belief system of worshipping the intellect. I wanted to go to a top university. I guess a part of me thought I would feel smarter or somehow be developed intellectually as a result of the process. How foolish I was!

I should have put an end to this insanity after my second master's degree in education. Unfortunately, I was only able to do it when I had left my human body and became aware that my Light Self was not human, not a biological being, a male, a female, or Black. In fact, I was aware that I was a genius, and have always been. It was that day that I realized that I was also definitely being duped through the education system. In May of 2009, after my spiritual experiences, I stopped in front of Carman Hall at Lehman College to consider my insane economic and educational decisions. As a result, I dropped out of my third master's degree program. The brainwashing had come to an abrupt end.

The 2009-2010 academic school year was like much of the previous years—Antoinette and my assistant principal still had every intention of screwing me despite the fight I had put up ten months thither.

The audacity of abuse!

What the assistant principal was doing was flat out intentional and given that she had been doing it for the sixth year, I considered it dark. During the ensuing academic school year, Kathy once again overloaded me with five preparations. This time, she gave me the duty period off. Despite my complaints to the union, nothing was done. I suppose I was not firm enough.

A few days before the 2009-2010 academic school started, I called Antoinette on her cell phone to see if she could work something out with me.

"…At least you have a job…," she said, I suppose as a way of pacifying me. However, her tone of voice betrayed her. I was in my new apartment in Rockland County, in the process of losing my house, I had lost my fiancée, I could not have given a shit about "at least having a job." I instinctively knew that a major part of her was bull-shitting me.

I called the other assistant principal at the second high school and began with:

"I've spoken to Kathy at…I have six preps—"

"That's too much!" she said, pleasantly interrupting me. Unlike Kathy at my main school, I sensed care in her voice. In fact, she even called me back to discuss the possible options she was working on.

Fortunately, the changes were made and my schedule was split between the two high schools. I enjoyed the schedule because it afforded me the opportunity to get some fresh air when I drove from one high school to the other.

The first semester passed with some pleasant and unpleasant surprises. I was pleased to see my chairperson observing the changes in my personality. She conveyed this during our post observation for the year.

"There's something different about you. You seem more confident."

"It's not about confidence. It's about knowing who you are beyond the mundane. The world is nothing like we think. It's really magical."

I looked at her, as if gauging her awareness.

"You're more experienced," she said, trying another avenue to understand me.

I have always admired her straightforwardness whether I agreed or disagreed with her. However, every which way she turned, she was blocked—she was trying to understand me through mundane means.

"It's not about religion or science or any of this mundane stuff. There is a love that cannot falter that reaches Infinity—you."

She had a quizzical look on her immobile face.

The semester passed without much incident. I continued working hard. I tutored after school for hours, helping students who sought not only extra help, but who had personal problems and were falling behind. In hindsight, I find that I was still working too hard. This general, genuine quality that I have nearly got me into trouble toward the beginning or the middle of the third quarter.

During my morning preparation period, the assistant principal Kathy called me into her office about a student who was not attending classes regularly because of personal issues. She recently had a baby and was very behind in her school work. She came to see me and I offered her additional tutoring hours. I even offered her a ride home once because of her babysitting situation where she could not get home on time. I helped because I thought I was doing the right thing. However, Kathy did not see my response that way.

"I want to talk to you about something," she began, taking out her notes, "There is no letter put in your file."

She was nonchalant without looking at me.

"Letter?" I frowned, "What?"

"You gave a ride to Mag…"

I was a little taken aback, thinking about how she found out. When I had volunteered to tutor and administer an exam to a male student at *his* house, I was not called into her office then.

"What kind of society are we living in where we can't help someone because of some arbitrary rule?"

"It's insurance," she said.

"I don't understand. I give people rides all the time. People give their friends a ride all the time and they don't ask them if they have insurance."

"If she got hurt, then you'll be at fault."

I understood what she was saying, but I knew it came from a place of fear and blind rules that did not take other people's humanity into account. It was then that she called me naïve, though I do not recall her exact statement.

"How did you learn this?" I asked her.

"The house lady."

"The black woman I spoke to?"

"It might have been construed as something else…You're a young black man…"

She could see that I was not buying any of her arguments and was becoming visibly annoyed.

"You even held and fed the baby!" she said with excitement, lifting up a sheet on the pad of notebook. Everything she had said was true. Mag did ask me if I wanted to feed her baby boy a bottle of milk. The black woman who was probably in her forties greeted me when

Mag and I entered the group home. She presented herself quite friendly. However, this apparent cordiality was fake, for it was the same woman who called to complain about me to the principal. It was the principal who asked the assistant principal Kathy to have a talk with me. I definitely recognize racism when I see it. Forget the fact that this woman is Black. Prejudices go beyond one's skin color, religion, science, and race. They are mostly inborn and to some extent unconscious. She had assumed that I was doing something immoral because I went to the group home.

"Where does it say in the contract that I can't help a student in need by giving her or him a ride?"

She had no answer for me because such a rule did not exist.

"We live in a society where our humanity is suppressed through fear. We live in a society where no matter who we put into power, the results are still the same. Look at Obama, what a disgrace…"

I was rambling and I knew it, though she was calm and collected, she could have cared less about what I was saying.

"If you want me not to give students rides, then I'll do it because you asked me, not because it is moral not to do so."

I did not tell her that I also gave several rides to other students including boys that she did not know about. I knew where she was coming from—a state of fear, which holds us back from doing the right thing because of society's slave rules.

Given that I told her that I would not give any other students rides, I kept my word for about a year or so. However, when I came to my senses, I ignored her.

After my meeting with Kathy, Antoinette also asked to talk to me. We were near the door in the foreign language office. I sat to the left of her desk. Unlike the assistant principal who did not ask about my side of the story, my chairperson began the conversation by asking me to tell her what happened.

"What if she turns around and accuses you of something? She would blame you."

"That's not my problem. All I have to do is to do the right thing. If she chooses the path of immorality, then that's on her. There's nothing I can do about that.

"If she lies, then she will have her chance to learn."

She was taken aback and was rendered to silence. I believe she sensed a spiritual conversation emerging. I knew she wanted to say more, but I believe she saw the futility in such a pursuit. I have to say that the difference between the two bosses was that Antoinette did not assume that I was guilty.

In November of 2010, something extraordinarily exciting happened that took my mind off the drama of my job.

I was driving back from the education course I was taking: "Discipline with Dignity." I was on the highway. I was thinking about the time I exited my physical vehicle to defend my body and mind from inter-dimensional and lower world entities. I was with form—light, nearly without weight. Then, quickly now all I could remember was the unbelievable joy. My mind shifted back to the car. I was still driving. The feeling was overwhelming. It consumed my mind, my face, my private parts. I, I…I was in ecstasy; my mind embraced it. I was in an unknown world of orgasmic pleasure and could not comprehend its origin.

Was this simply thinking good thoughts? Remembering joys from the past?

It did not matter, for I really liked it. The feeling remained all the way with me until I pulled into the parking lot at my residence.

Being joyous without knowing why.

I wanted more. It was like having sex with the most beautiful girl ever while drinking red wine at the same time. This incident would later change my understanding of the nature of sensual pleasure.

In December of 2010, my mind was back to our control system of work and the control of our resources. It was the 22nd and I was having a conversation with my job's mechanical repairman that nicely linked the economic and education systems for me. At the end of my last class, an older white male walked into my classroom carrying white blinds and reparation tools.

"Oh, cool, you're putting up blinds."

I walked to the left side of the window. I put my finger to the crevice. I felt the air creeping through my fingers even though the window was closed.

"They are not well insulated," I said, looking at the window. I walked toward him.

"Happy Thursday, tomorrow is Friday."

It was really Wednesday, but since we did not have school on Friday, I optimistically referred to Wednesday as Thursday and Thursday as Friday. I do not even remember how the conversation started, but before I knew it we were talking about America and the world. I recall asking him about debt and retirement. He answered that he was doing alright and that his children for the most part had scholarships and he and his wife had helped them. He said that things were not so bad. I was curious.

"But you still have to work until you're sixty-five years old. By then you are more or less ready to die. You know, California is trying to raise the retirement age to 69. There is fundamentally something wrong that is compelling us to work until we are ready to die."

He asked me if I had tenure. I answered affirmatively. He smiled and said to enjoy it.

"Most of the teachers are rushing out of here as soon as school is over…Americans are lazy."

I smiled wondrously.

"Seriously, I am not quite sure. Most people have two or three jobs in order to survive. It's not like France where there is a 35-hour work week. Even there, people are suffering. I may be talking too much, but I don't understand the economic system. The system doesn't make any sense. It's all basically the same fundamentally, whether it is capitalism, socialism, or communism. The puppet master gives the illusion of a difference between them. The differences between them are superficial at best."

He listened attentively as he put up the blinds.

"This one is too short," he said.

"Banks don't create wealth. The Central Bank prints money out of thin air, which is not backed up by anything. It's a total fraud, and we the people allow it. Can you imagine being in charge of an institution and just faking or making things up? A teacher-friend told me something that I will never forget."

"What's that?" he asked.

"Real wealth comes from two sources: we human beings actually working and Mother Earth. These major banks are legal gangsters colluding with the government to keep us as slaves. In what world or consciousness does it make sense for a soul to work until *It* is sixty-five or sixty-nine years old when It knows that he or she is eternal. A third of the money is used to build armies to kill our so-called enemies, in order to protect us? Get out of here!"

He cut me off. He was full of information now. He spoke and spoke about "Mesa Energy and fracking."

At first, I remained quiet, trying to understand what "fracking" was. However, after about a minute when he did not say precisely, I asked him.

"What's fracking?" As soon as I had asked, I answered my own question with, "Oh, to fracture, to break."

"There are oil resource reserves underneath the ground, but the people who own the land are not allowed to drill. There are all these laws. You can't drill within 200 miles."

"What? I didn't know about this," I said slightly frowning, and jotting down "Mesa Energy" on a piece of paper.

"You see, this is what I am talking about. The resources are there. Why is it that the government has such a tight hold on our natural resources? Why is that only big companies and the government who control them? We are not human beings having an experience, but souls temporarily sojourning in this realm. Everything belongs to everybody. We're all connected. We're slaves. This is total slavery without boundaries or bars."

"Yes, slavery is the right word," he said.

"I don't even understand why I am paid to work. To survive? Why do I have to work to survive? I don't get it! We are eternal, yet we have to work to survive temporarily?"

"People get accustomed to things," he said.

I sensed that he was understanding the majority of what I was saying, and that was good enough for me, because most people I have come across since my spiritual awakening, did not understand much of what I said.

"Yeah, but we don't have to live like this. It's amazing. Most people are awe-struck when I say that their souls are in their bodies."

I looked at the clock. It was getting late.

"I have to get going. It has been great talking to you. What is your name?" I put my right hand forward for him to shake.

"Doug," he answered.

"The kids call me Mr. Epou, but my first name is Agbe." As I walked toward the main office, I thought about how fruitful the conversation had been. Yet, the underlying question of the current economic system compelled me to debate the whole thing some more in my mind. *What is money?* I heard myself saying that it is a means of an exchange. That was what I had been taught in my economic classes. I was understanding much more than the banal things I had learned in my economic programs as an undergraduate and graduate student. The monetary system as it is set up now makes absolutely no sense. It is part of a system that keeps people in fear. I was thinking about this when I entered the foreign language office.

There are different types of banks—investment banks, the bond market, commercial banks. They all sell debt which never existed in the first place. Only a portion of this really exists—what the average person puts into the banks to begin with. The rest is fake. Take the fractional reserve system as an example. Banks loan out money they never had and will never have. This is the reason why we have such things as run on banks. Presidents come and go—and they support the same insane economic system. So, please tell me what the difference really is between a Republican and a Democrat when they are both supporting the same crazy slave-system? None!

People are dying because of debt. Let us consider the insanity of the debt system for the individual. A typical American gets out of college so indebted that he or she must pay several hundred dollars on a monthly basis. On top of that, there are mortgage payments, which when one is finished paying is about two and a half times the cost of the actual purchase price of the house. Half of this is interest on a loan, which has been created out of thin air. Then, of course the individual must pay for his or her children's education. The Ivy league schools are now between $30-60 thousand dollars a year. Let us not forget that most Americans make less than $50,000 a year. With all these impediments, when can you really own anything? You can't purchase land or a house in most "developed" countries without some sort of a permanent tax strangle. So, fellow citizens, please tell me when you really own anything in North America, Europe or other parts of the developed world? Please don't say that people own their houses. They don't. I have friends who are paying about twenty thousand dollars in taxes a year. They can never stop paying. What possible reason can you give me for all these taxes and forms of enslavement? I can already imagine some people defending this insane system. Well, one of my colleagues did. Let us go into this.

A week or so before we took our Christmas break in 2010, I was in my main classroom with the door open, and preparing my lesson plans when one of my staff members, Latticha, walked into the room to make a phone call. I raised my head slowly from the desk. She looked downtrodden.

"Overworking again?" I inquired.

"Yeah," she said sadly, "I've told you, I have two jobs."

"What time do you start this one?"

"6:30."

"And the other one?"

"At 3 o'clock; until 11 p.m. I don't see my children."

"Wow! You can't do that forever. You are a slave."

"That's exactly what it is. Slavery without bars," she said, taking the words right out of my mouth. I was pleasantly surprised that she understood, for most people I come across do not understand that they have accepted their slavery.

Latticha was on the phone now. When she got off, I told her that maybe it would be a good idea to purchase some land to farm or something. Then I paused.

"Unless farmland is taxed. I know that Texas and Florida don't have taxes, either income or property."

"I think farmland is taxed," she said.

"Even if you pay for it completely and don't have any loans?"

"I think so," she said, "Let me ask Mr. Bob. He should know."

Bob, which is not his real name, was a tall social studies teacher, and he was sitting outside to the right of my classroom. Latticha asked him, and his answer was yes. Latticha left to do her rounds, and I finished going over my lesson plans. As I exited the room, I could not help but strike up a conversation with Bob.

"So you're saying that landowners have to pay taxes on the land they wholly own? Get out of here!"

"Well, you need public services like the fire department. If you own land there, you have access to community water…Those things aren't free."

"Why shouldn't they be?" I asked, challenging him, "Why should we be paying to live on a planet that we own? I don't get it. The world is looking more and more the same. People are just surviving. Countries have natural resources in the ground. Shouldn't that belong to everyone? Who put the government or big business in charge of these resources? You're telling me that these resources can't be used for everyone? To pay for such things as fire services? Really?"

"I understand your philosophical view on this, and I agree….What are you proposing communism…?"

"I am not proposing anything. I just want us to stick to the main point of the discussion here. Communism, capitalism, Socialism you mentioned to me are of no importance. In the end, you get the same result—a lack of freedom. I am talking about paying attention to one's basic instincts."

Before I knew it, he was attempting to change the focus of the conversation by making it a personal matter.

"How long have you been at the job—"

"This is not about me," I said, already knowing what he was thinking, "It's not a personal matter. Look at Latticha, she's working two jobs just to survive, if that isn't imprisonment I don't know what is."

"Well, you need the education to get paid more…No one ever dies from starvation in America."

I was silent for a brief second, considering his statement. I knew it was flawed, but wanted to think about it. I realized that I had to let the conversation go or else I was not going to get anything done during my two preparation periods. He too realized this.

"At some point one has to ask oneself if one has a soul or not," I said passing the bathroom on the right. I caught a cold breeze from the double door on my left. A look somewhere between a frown and puzzlement etched up his face. It was clear to me that we were in two different worlds. His back was resting against the wall.

Despite our different sense of awareness of the mundane, I would consider his comments about starvation and education for a long time. I completely understood his point of view, for I used to think the same way. This way of thinking has been instilled in us from birth. Basically, we are told that America is the land of opportunity and you can succeed by working hard and having a good education. But Reader, please consider my comment about having a soul.

Most of what we teachers are teachings students is not essential for the growth of the soul. The things that should be emphasized should be conflict resolution, solving problems, traditional medicine, how to reduce violence, avoiding war, exploring what the soul is, better nutrition that is more organic-based, soul development, the Self beyond culture, race, religion, and so forth. These things are either not taught or some are superficially treated in the curriculum.

"Go talk to….he is an expert in economics," I said

"I have a master's degree in economics," I said softly, staring at him.

I went into the office and that was the end of the conversation.

I began thinking about the formal education again. This system was set up around the world to worship the mind, the intellect. Recall what I said about that day I was out of my physical body and many times thereafter. I was far more intelligent than my mind, the intellect. I had capabilities that Superman could only ever dare imagine. I knew I was a genius and school was a complete manipulation—a fraud. This sense of being a genius pertained to all beings. I immediately understood that the intellect is superficial. Thus, I began asking myself: *Why are we torturing our children with superficial knowledge that do not allow them to reach the highest part of themselves?* Is it any wonder children sometimes say, "Why do we have to learn this?" Well, sometimes our children are right. Given this insight that we possess beauty and intellect far more than we are aware of as human beings, why should Latticha be pursuing a formal education that doesn't help her soul develop? I will bet she has acquired more insight about the nature of existence than most people with master's degrees and PhDs. This was the reason why I dropped out of the master's degree program in education administration. The program was not teaching me anything practical that I could take with me to the next dimension of existence.

My colleague's other comment was that no one ever starves to death in America. After much reflection and research, I could not disagree more. A few years ago, I recall watching a television show about families starving in a very poor neighborhood in Camden, New Jersey. I recall a mother struggling to feed her children, living on one meal a day and sleeping in the most atrocious living conditions. One particular family with several children only had one bed in a single room, which was often flooded. In addition, their mother was in danger of losing the room because she could not afford to pay the rent. I do not know if the woman and her children starved to death, but what is the real difference between enduring such a situation and dying from starvation? Death would be a release. Reader, be mindful that death doesn't really exist because the Light Body or the Soul will always survive. The worse thing in any consciousness or existence is suffering, not death from actual starvation. As you embark on this journey with me, you will see the awful truth of what I mean.

In June 2011, my mind opened up more spiritually and my desire to *stop* the foolishness around me reached its pinnacle.

Kathy was back to her old tricks. There was less than a month left of school and as a result the ensuing year teaching schedules had to be created. As usual, she gave me more than four preparations. This time I knew I could *stop* her.

A meeting was set up with the other French teacher and the assistant principal Kathy to discuss the teaching schedule for the next academic school year. We discussed how we could rearrange the schedule such that I would have three preparations and did not see any possible way to do it within the high school.

"Even if I give you…you'll still have four preps. It's the nature of the French program."

This was definitely a cop-out.

"You can consider the split option," I said, "You can tell the district that this option will reduce the number of preps."

"I'll send them an e-mail," she said.

I thought that she would inform the district; however, I knew that she would not push for me to be split between the two high schools. She wanted to keep me where I was because I had good results even though she did not appreciate me.

On June 9, 2011, my other French colleague e-mailed Kathy at 10:47 a.m.

> I have been assigned French IV Advanced and French IV AP as separate assignments. Agbe Epou has been assigned French V Advanced and V AP. We decided with Antoinette a couple of years ago that combining the AP and Advanced students at this level simply doesn't work. Both groups are compromised. The Advanced students simply cannot keep up with the AP kids, and the thrust of the class is highly academic gearing to the AP Exam and not what the Advanced students are looking for in an elective. So we changed it to Advanced IV and Advanced V together. If you switch the AP IV to Agbe, I could teach the Beg.2 which is one of my preferences. Your thoughts and can we discuss?

At 12:21 p.m. on the same day, Kathy wrote:

> Hi Dona, I just reviewed it with Melissa and the assignment should be as follows: Dona: 2 classes of IV ADV/IV AP combined, 2 classes of French II, 1 class of IIH. Agbe: 1 class of Beginning 2, 1 class of IV/V AP combines, 2 classes of IIIR, 1 class IIIH. Unfortunately we do not have enough staffing to separate the AP and Advanced classes.

On June 10, 2011 at 2:51 p.m. I wrote the following e-mail to Kathy:

> Thank you for the update. This arrangement seems better for the students. However, I still have some concerns. Would it be possible to schedule a meeting to discuss it? Also, could we still pursue the split option to reduce the number of preps?
>
> Sincerely,
>
> Agbe

Reader, please notice the words “split option” in the above message.

At 3:04 p.m. of the same day, Kathy wrote:

> I have already reached out to Personnel regarding your concerns for the split. Believe me, I understand your concerns about AP and Advanced being mixed, since I have gone through it myself. There is really no other option at this point.

As my battle with the abuse at work continued, so would my experiences into the world of the "unknown."

During the second week of June 2011, I raised my right hand to wipe my face of what felt like spider webs. It was during the eighth period class, and I was in the middle of teaching French 3. I had been on the same spot for at least two minutes, so I knew that the webs came out of nowhere.

"What are you doing Mr. Epou?" the slim Black Haitian-American female student asked.

"Nothing," I must have said with a perplexed look, "I just have this thing in my face."

Several weeks later while preparing to administer the listening section of the French Regents exam, the same thing happened.

"Mr. Epou, there's nothing there."

"It's a spider web," I said to her.

She smiled in disbelief.

"Let's get started with the test," I said.

CHAPTER 4

HOLISTIC HEALING THROUGH FOOD AND PLANT MEDICINE

In 2009 when the invisible became visible, I was forced to confront my insane stupidity. I began seeking none traditional help. One of the places that I went to was Cuernavaca, Mexico. I asked my host mother to help me find someone who could take the "objects" or "things" out of my body. Somehow or another, the lady she recommended was always unavailable. When she finally got back to me, it was too late, for I was going to depart in a few days. However, she did leave an interesting message.

"Everything that has to do with taking things out of the body is done orally."

I was mostly sure she knew what she was talking about. Nevertheless, I was positive there was an exception to spiritual healing. At that time I was looking into two traditional plant medicines—Ayahuasca and Peyote. My research into these two traditional plants indicated that they were at the top of the plant pyramid. I had already made up my mind to try Ayahuasca first to see if it would heal me. It is called the God vine, or the God of all plants. It is actually a brew or a tea made from two plants. It is supposed to cure major and minor illnesses: physical, emotional, and spiritual.

The major countries that use it are Peru, Brazil, Columbia…It is illegal in the United States under the pretext that it is dangerous. Well, I personally no longer believe that. I believe that natural drugs serve as a gateway to open up one's mind and to know one's Light Self. I was also intrigued by this tea because of its spiritual nature. Some who have taken it have said that they have spoken to their loved ones who have passed. The plant supposedly also gives you spiritual protection against negative energy and entities.

I had the idea that somehow these plants would help me vomit out these things in my body.

In terms of Peyote, I really did not know much about the medicine. I read and watched some testimonial videos about it.

Once I understood that there were not any negative side effects, I was determined to try both of these traditional medicines if the healers in Mexico and Togo could not help me, but first I had to save some money to take the trips across the continents.

As I saved the money for the trips, I revisited the problem I was having eating certain types of foods. Sometime on the weekend in September of 2009, I went to the supermarket, Top Tomato in Westchester to do my grocery shopping. Actually, the main reason why I displaced myself and drove there was to purchase some okra from this store. You don't understand Reader, I love eating okra stew and sauce with akple. I grew up eating it. You see, it just did not make any sense for one to have been eating a certain type of food all of one's life, then all of a sudden one day be told that one could no longer eat it because it did not agree with one's stomach. I wanted to understand the cause of this problem.

As I mentioned before, I first noticed the food problem in 2007 with my stomach tormenting me. Then in August of 2009, a voodoo psychic in Lomé told me that my stomach problem was a result of some of the food I was eating. I was told not to eat "sticky" or high starch food like cassavas, yams, and okras. For the most part, I listened to the advice, but was not satisfied with his inability to explain to me how, I, all of a sudden developed this aversion to these food.

In any case, I was definitely going to ignore their advice on that Saturday afternoon when I returned from the Westchester store. I made one of the most delicious stew sauces ever. It had plenty of mushrooms and sautéed onions. When the stew was almost ready, I let it simmer on the stove while I used some cassava floor to cook the akple. I ate it with appetite.

That evening and the next, I waited for my stomach to hurt. It did not. I rationalized it. The soup was not thick with "stickiness." I was trying to understand what was really causing the stomach problem.

A few days later, I began thinking that just maybe I was overcoming the problem. I thus decided to make some tapioca. I ate it and nothing happened. I saved the leftovers for the ensuing day for breakfast. After eating breakfast, my stomach began to hurt.

That evening, like most evenings, my stomach problem impeded my sleep. It grumbled constantly at night. In addition, I was constantly passing gas in the most usual places.

It was then that I decided to go to the organic food store *A Matter of Health* to talk to their doctors. I told the first doctor about my gas problem. He told me not drink water with my meals. I had been drinking water with my meals as long as I could remember, but I did not have this problem. I gave him the benefit of the doubt, but something told me that he was not making sense. I knew that there was more to my problems than simply not drinking water.

A day or two later, I returned to the same supermarket. I was in the vitamin and herbal section of the organic food supermarket. I was not finding what I came for. That was when I turned and saw an old White man who was a medical specialist.

"I can't fall asleep. Where can I find some remedy?"

He was looking at me in the most interesting way.

"It's two aisles up, to the right."

As soon as I began walking away, Walter said the oddest of things.

"You have the weight of the world on your shoulders."

I turned and looked with a slight perplexed countenance. He followed and helped me pick some melatonin and something else, which I do not recall.

A few days later, I returned to inform him that the medicine did not work and that I had to return to my organic red wine.

"It's the only thing that works, but it's too expensive. I really don't want to return to none organic red wine. I hear alcohol kills brain cells. Is that true?"

"Yes, that's why they use it on wounds."

He walked over to the left side of the medicinal aisle.

"Try these…"

"You have good energy about you, and you're old."

He looked at me with none-biased eyes, trying to understand. I had to go, so I left that day without explaining to him what I meant.

I returned again a few days later to inform him once again that his remedies did not work.

"It's alright. I'll stick to my red wine for now. Listen, I don't think you understood what I meant when I said that you are old. This is a good thing. Death is not real. I am a little envious. The world is really magical. We live in what should be a magical dimension. So many lies and manipulations!"

He smiled.

"We merely pass on. You can't imagine what I have seen…I am between dimensions…," he said.

Before I knew it, we were deeply involved in a none-traditional passionate and sweet discussion. It was comforting to find someone who understands. He spoke about his experiences and I listened attentively retaining his every word.

"…fallen angels are real."

"You don't have to convince me of that. They're just like us, but have made the wrong decisions. Their aura is literally dark," I added.

He agreed, then suddenly a question popped into my mind about auras. Before I could verbalize the question, he gave me the answer.

"Yours is lavender, which is really the best kind."

I can't remember if he actually said "lavender" or purple."

"Get out of here! You have the visual access to perceive auras?"

The auric field is the none-visual energy field that surrounds our bodies.

The conversations with this guy were so exquisite that whenever I went to the store, I looked for him. Our last conversation was most intriguing.

"You know so much," I said to him, "Why don't you write a book about it. It could help us in the fight against the global slave system.

"I am not supposed to," he answered to my astonishment.

"What do you mean you're not supposed to? I chose to write this book," referring to A Glimpse of Who We Are, which I was editing on my laptop computer when he came to say hello.

"You *did* receive a message to write it. You're just not aware of it."

I must have paused for a few eternal seconds to consider his pronouncement before saying, "What?" with a slight frown.

Who is this guy?

"My job for now is to be here giving medical advice..."

I found his answer fascinating.

We each have different roles to play in raising the positive consciousness of Infinity. No task is trivial.

"Work away. I can't wait to read it," he said with a smile and enthusiasm.

I saw him once again briefly, and then he seemed to have disappeared. Though I would go to the store constantly to buy food, I would never see him again.

About a month elapsed. My awareness sharpened to the point where I intuitively understood that I needed to change my diet. It was evident to me that that there is an intimate relationship between what we put in our bodies and *how* we *feel*. I wanted to get rid of all forms of anxieties and worries that did not emanate from my ultimate Light Self. Thus, I began paying attention to details. I paid attention to the labeling of food in supermarkets such as ShopRite or Costco or wherever I shopped. When I saw food labeled "natural" I read the ingredients carefully. It is not *natural* that the vast majority of what we eat is chemically and genetically altered for the worse.

Today, I heard a story that I found quite interesting. A young woman of 25 years of age discovered that she had cancer and decided to change her eating habit. After several years of eating nothing but organic food, the cancer disappeared. At this point, you may be thinking that the disappearance of the cancer may be due to other reasons. I agree with this. However, I would add that this is an example of a soul realizing that there is absolutely something wrong with the crap she was being fed. It is no accident that we cannot go to a restaurant that serves none-chemical free food. There is a reason why there are a lot of medications out there. There is a reason why Americans are so obese. It is not merely because Americans eat too much fat food. The key is in the seed. Every plant, fruit, and vegetable has a seed. Corrupt the seed, and voilà, you have an unnatural crop. If you are thinking Monsanto and other corporations that produce genetically modified food, then you are on the right track. They propagate lies and manipulate the public in believing that the crap they provide to the average supermarket is safe, when it is completely unsafe and pernicious in the long term for human consumption. The cereal box is healthier than the cereal itself. But, then again, I myself would not fully feel the truth of this for a few months to come.

At this stage of being my own scientist, I was still a little insecure, for I still considered the whole protein argument a valid reason for eating meat and fish. The main rational for killing animals for protein is that vegetarians are putting themselves in a health bind "because they do not consume enough protein." I read the most fear-based postings on the internet. Some people claimed that vegetarians' insufficient consumption of protein would lead to a built up of diseases overtime. This would "supposedly" result in a shorter life span. Some of these people even said that they tried to be vegetarians for several months and even a year, and were unsuccessful because they became extremely depressed, and as a result, they had to switch back to eating meat. I took these statements seriously, but a part of me knew that these people were still caught up in the "mind." They were afraid of death. I recall one blogger saying that if it were between the animal's life and hers, the animal had to die.

Over several days, I searched the internet and books about how much protein the body really needs per day. Most of what I came across mentioned something like 70 grams a day. I started consuming none meat and none fish food that were high in protein, but the total was not quite adding up to 70. Then, I had an idea. I decided to research the food pyramid and its validity. I found several articles stating that the food pyramid is a fraud, promoted by global corporations. Further research indicated that the human body really only needs 3 percent of protein intake per meal. Finally, I came across a wonderful mainstream research that indicated that the human body produces 59% of its own nutrients including protein. This proved that the protein myth was fear-based to keep us eating as much meat as possible. I wanted to know if this were really true, so after about a year and a half of not eating meat or fish, I went to take a blood test. The blood test indicated that my protein level was extremely high. It was then that I lost my faith in general supermarkets. I took organic fruit and vegetables vitamins of course. I was to quickly understand that most of the American food supply is being controlled by one global corporation—Monsanto. Monsanto is a company that has somehow convinced the Federal Department of Agriculture that its genetically modified food is alright for human consumption.

In the early months of 2009, I began understanding that the overall human food supply is poisonous. I was aware that food could aid me in escaping from the Third Dimension. Thus, I stopped eating genetically modified food altogether; for I understand the connection between the physical and the none-physical body! To understand this, one must first understand the nature of energy. As I said at the beginning of this book, energy is not really physical. When one puts physical food in one's body, one's system breaks it down into little pieces. However, the physical pieces must be dissolved into an apparent nothingness. This nothingness isn't really nothing. It is energy. Physical food is merely one type of energy.

Now, let us come to an obvious connection: The real essence of food is not physical at all, and we know that our ultimate Light Self is also not physical. It is at this level that food affects the soul.

By 2009, I was completely aware that there is a connection between food and the tremendous physical, mental and spiritual suffering that I had endured. My intuition compelled me to reconsider the nature of food. I had the intuitive experience knowing that there are layers of each person. The outer layer is the most physical. Food is also physical. I understood that when one puts, lets us say a piece of cooked chicken one's physical vehicle, it has an effect in the composition of the body. Furthermore, I understood that meat was dense, heavy like the physical body. It was at this point that I really understood at the intuitive level the common expression "You are what you eat." Food literally affects how you feel physically, emotionally, mentally, and spiritually. On the physical level, it affects your internal organs. It goes from physical to none physical, finally getting to your Light Being. This thus affects your emotional, mental, and spiritual well-being. Because of the density of meat, it holds the soul in a low state of awareness. In short, consuming higher conscious beings who can feel like us, diminishes our overall perception of the nature of things.

The spiritual element of my development was another great reason to cease eating meat and fish. Once I stopped for several months, I regained an immense state of tranquility.

My desire to escape from this planet had reached its climax. About a month after giving up meat, I also gave up eating fish. Merely a few months after quitting this bad eating habit, the web of worldly deception was quickly fading away. My own blindness was becoming increasingly clear to me. I was more and more willing to analyze myself—past and present. I understood that this was cleansing, healing, and finally freeing myself from the world slave system. It was clear to me that escaping from the third dimension requires much diligence in terms of what we consume. By far, the biggest thing I am doing is watching what I eat. Food is so important, yet so many of us do not pay attention to what we put in our bodies. Until my spiritual awakening, I did not really feel the importance of this. I think it was because I was too busy paying attention to the collective unconscious. I adopted the average person's food consumption practice. Now that I reflect back on my life, there were moments when my Light Self spoke to me through feelings and symbolism.

One of those moments was the summer of my third year in college at the University of the Pacific. I was working as a student residential assistant and as a result had to share an apartment with two other students. One afternoon, I had sautéed some chicken for a late lunch with onions. I was really looking forward to the meal. But, I was momentarily held to the spot. I stood near the stairs leading to the second floor. A wave of discomfort swept through my entire being. I stood on the spot, confused, but most importantly feeling sad for the chicken I was about to consume. Images of days of old came *whooshing* down my mind. I saw myself killing chickens in Togo, West Africa. On one particular occasion I cut a hen's throat, but it was not a clean cut. She bounced on the ground every which way.

Presently, I turned my eyes towards my plate of food and stared at the chicken. I held the meat down in a stabbing, straight position for a second or two considering the plight of the being. Finally, I cut the meat and took a piece to my mouth. I held it near my mouth's entrance. My face went blank. The feeling that had a hold of me earlier was still strong. I put my fork down. Try as I might, I could not eat the meat. The ensuing day, I again had difficulty eating flesh. By the third day, the immense feeling that overtook me wore off. I was back to being a carnivore. That was not a good feeling.

About ten years later, this terrible feeling returned after I left my physical body many times in a span of four months. During the fifth month, the feeling of sadness that I experienced in college turned into guilt. The guilt was so strong that one day I halted my action of cutting through the whole chicken that I bought at ShopRite. At that moment, memories of my childhood ram animal-friend etched upon my mind. My consumption of meat became infrequent, but nevertheless it did not cease for another two and a half months. I substituted fish for meat.

I must say that my spiritual journey has been mostly a lonely road. I have not had much support, especially in the meat department. I have found it frustrating and fear-based. Let us first look at the frustration.

In Mexico, I was told that I didn't eat meat because of my big ego. This was said with passion and intensity. I did not say anything in return to the woman, for I was too taken aback. Even those who on the surface appeared neutral had their silent harsh disapproval. One of them who was very religious, said with a calm voice:

"It's just a choice."

I was in the Teachers' Lounge at work, making photocopies. By then, I had had enough of these haters. I turned around, looked at her and said:

"It's a damn good spiritual decision."

She said nothing more. I mean, these haters were too much. It was not like I was asking them to stop eating meat. What was surprising was the extent of their negativity. Even when I used to eat meat I was not negative toward vegetarians. If anything, I did not make much of an effort to understand them. I recall a parent at Columbia University vehemently expressing his opinion with a scolding demeanor as he said to me, "They're just like us!" I was silent, trying to *understand* his passionate declaration, trying to understand him, but I did not get angry at his authoritative, harsh tone.

In hindsight, I believe the hateful energy that some people displayed toward me was due to their hidden inability to listen to their own conscious. I also believe that a part of them secretly wished they could do what I was doing. Sometimes when the battle is too great, we often take refuge in denial and other lesser authorities other than the purest part of ourselves. If it is not religious texts, then it is scientific or cultural. We will find anything to placate our actions.

Escaping from the Third Dimension also entailed healing my physical and spiritual bodies. In terms of spirituality, recall that I said earlier that I still have something or things in my body that are manifesting themselves in my physical body. The negative energy or objects in my body have been reduced somewhat because of the physical and spiritual actions I have taken. The change in what I eat is a tremendous help.

Recently, I decided to try acupuncture as well. I had three meetings with the doctors. I showed them two videos that I recorded of the palpitations during our first meeting. After the consultations, the doctors stuck needles in the crevices of my left and right arms and my feet. There was a little bit of change in my body.

During the second session, the doctor used even more needles. He stuck them in the center of my head, my right arm, and my feet. The result was another slight decrease in the palpitations. By the third session, I told him to go right to the source of the problem. He was alright with this, so he placed needles in my left neck area, right above my heart, my biceps and the center of the head. As a result, there was a noticeable decrease in the palpitations in my left chest. Nevertheless my triceps, biceps, feet, and buttocks were still palpitating. It was as if there were a war going on inside my body.

To fight the war inside my body and the intrusion on my *Mind*, I had to reconsider everything society taught me about drugs. I began with the popular belief that all drugs are dangerous and can "mess with" and damage your brain. I used the internet as a guide to research basic drugs contents and their effects on the physical body. I even came across a a CIA whistleblower who actually had papers explaining how the war on drugs is a fraud. That was just the beginning. At this point, I decided to research traditional medicine. I quickly found out that plant brews such as Ayahuasca had no negative effect on the brain whatsoever. In fact, I would later discover for myself that it is a fantastic detox aid. As a result, I saw a connection between how medicine is controlled through the so-called experts—doctors. The medical system is tightly regulated. The last time I went to the doctor for a blood test, I had to get permission from this and that doctor "expert." I thought to myself: *For the love of God, I'm an adult. Why such a stringent system of control? These doctors have become scientific Gods of our time.* Recall that I had a message in 2009 that said that we are literally a piece of God, and if such a declaration is true, then why the elaborate system of permission? It did not make any sense.

The hidden reason for the control of our health system is far more than keeping us safe through these so-called doctor experts. There is a larger agenda to control our physical, mental and spiritual health. There has never been a war on drugs. In fact, if you do a bit of research, you will quickly discover that it is no accident that the mainstream media constantly demonizes drug use as shameful and people who use it as criminals. Intelligence agencies such as the CIA lump street drugs such as heroine, crack, and cocaine with traditional medicinal plants as the same. The CIA infiltrates countries to spread dangerous street drugs. Having been exposed to this, I quickly made a larger connection to the reason why good drugs are illegal in most "developed" countries: The most senior level of governments around the world ban drugs because their use allows people to know not only who they are, but gives them spiritual protection against the dark arts as well as global corporations' hypnotic suggestions through advertisements.

There is a correlation between the ban on traditional medicine as part of the overall slave system. Traditional plant medicine or drugs allow you to see what is possible in the universe beyond the limited five senses—the Infinite possibility of ourselves. Drugs serve to open up the gateway to the different layers that comprise that each human being in physical form. The mind doesn't play "tricks." Once I became aware of this, the speed with which I advanced toward my freedom knew no limits.

CHAPTER 5

MY LINGERING ETERNAL QUESTIONS

Perchance it is because I have booked reservations for my mother and I to go to the Amazon to cleanse our bodies by taking Ayahuasca, or perhaps it is because I wanted to know why I had suffered so much. Whatever the truth may be, my thirst to find answers to life's biggest mysteries and to be free intensified. In the last few months, my lingering intents as they have manifested through my thoughts have taken over my daily preoccupation. I have spent hours a day at work and at home brooding over such intents.

As I analyze myself now, I understand that the law of attraction has always been at work through all of my frustrations, sadness for my brother's loss, my childhood pains in California, my smiles and laughter. The law of attraction has helped me to become aware of the fact that I have always yearned to understand how individuals and nations can protect themselves without the use of negative energy (i.e., violence). I wanted to know how reincarnation really works throughout the universe. I also wanted to know how vegetables perceive. Lastly, I wanted to know my purpose on this planet. I recall the exact moments in my life where I can tell you where the intensity of my desires manifested its will.

One such time was in California. I recall being in a fair of some sort. I vividly remember having a worldly discussion with my Afghanistan-American friend about the chaos in the world. He was about three years older than me. I don't recall my exact words to him, but I remember his exact words to me.

"You do these things in Africa, then what? What does that do?"

There was a sense of defeat in his voice, and the tone and resonance manifested it. It indicated that one could not change the world. I became quiet, and disappointed at his defeated attitude. Then my brother's moonwalk dance came to my mind. A series of images of my brother at Center High School in California made me smile. We were standing by the weight room, hanging out. There were a few girls and boys. My brother Essevi started doing the moon dance. I watched him, amazed, for the imitation seemed as good as the real Michael. I wanted to imitate his moves, but dared not.

Another occasion when the intensity of my desires manifested its positive will was when I was sitting in the army recruiter's office where he wanted me to enlist. As I sat there looking at a picture of what they wanted me to do in the military, I knew deep inside such physical violence was futile. I told them that I was a conscientious objector, and was eventually on my way home.

When I was in the 10th grade, I was applauded (in an evening award ceremony) for having written an inspiring essay about peace. When asked how I did it, I merely said that I bull-shitted, that I wrote what came to me. Then, there was also the time in college when I won a few hundred dollars for an essay that I wrote in French about Mother Earth and technological destruction on the planet. Again, the words came easily.

Finally, in the early years of 2000, I saw myself in the bus station at Silver Spring, Maryland. I was in the car with my mother and somehow, we were engaged in a conversation about Kwame Nkrumah, the so-called father of African nationalism. My mother listened attentively and shared her opinions about the problems ravaging Africa. When I spoke positively about Kwame, she pointed out with:

"He killed a lot of people."

My answer to her was:

"I need to discover that for myself. I'll keep reading."

What I was doing here became much clearer to me after my spiritual awakening in 2009. I was impressed by Kwame's lofty goals of freeing Ghana from the claws of the queen of England and her cronies. I also wanted to know how he was going to do this without the use of violence. After reading his secret manual which was seized by the European imperialists, I understood that Kwame Nkrumah was no hero. Neither was Jomo Kenyatta of Kenya. The only true African hero that I know of was Patrice Lumumba of the Congo.

By far the most important manifestation of the answer to my intents was a vision that I had about a place I had never been. There were tall and small green trees. I saw myself walking to and from somewhere with a handful of people in the forest of some sort. Slightly above, like another level of the forest was a woman. She seemed to be in her late twenties, medium height with dark hair, and had a reassuring smile—a knowing smile. I thought maybe this would be someone I would meet in Peru, for it has happened many times before.

When we were going the opposite direction from which we came on a particular path, a weird-feeling kicked in. It was doubt, fear-like, which was not spoken. It was a feeling akin to kidnapping. It was weird, for it was not at all synchronized with the rest of the vision. This same feeling of interference occurred with my 2007 airplane explosion vision. In that vision, I could never figure out the end, though I definitely knew there was one. The best word to describe these occurrences is "blockage."

Somehow in the forest vision I was being blocked and I knew this without a shadow of a doubt. As a part of my mind began to focus on the fear, the simple, but beautiful woman soothed me with her calm words.

"I'll meet you down there later."

For the ensuing months to come I would remember the smile of the beautiful woman, but a part of me could not help but question the vision, for there was something missing—the end. Try as I might, it would not come to me.

The last answer to the intents that I sent out to the universe came in a form of a dialogue with a middle-aged Haitian man while at work. He walked toward the exit of the main office of the high school. I opened it and waited for him to exit. He exited and thanked me.

"Pas de quoi," I said, letting him know it was not a big thing.

"What are you looking for?"

The Dean's Office," he answered.

"I'll take you."

I was on my preparation period, and had a few minutes to spare. When we reached the security guard, he shook my hand, thanked me and asked:

"You are nice. Are you a Christian?"

I sensed a spiritual conversation coming. I braced myself and anticipated his questions.

"No, I am not."

"What's your religion?"

"I have none."

"No?"

"Do you believe in God?"

"Believe?" I said, more like a statement than a question, "What human beings need to do is lose words like 'belief' when talking about Infinity."

"God exists!" he said passionately, "I was in the Haitian earthquake. Everything around me was destroyed, but I survived. I was safe among ruins."

"Understood," I said, "You survived because there was no lesson to learn in you losing your life. If there were a lesson in you dying, then your soul would have rendered itself to death," I said with firmness in French, for I did not want people around to get involved in this passionate conversation. One of my department colleagues sneaked a curious look at me. He did not speak much French. I continued.

"There is no such thing as death or even birth. It's like an illusion, but not really. Illusion is not even the correct word."

"Where are you from?"

"That won't help you."

His pupils became intensely focused on me with calm.

"Are you a magician?"

It was my turn to listen. His eyes held mine with steadiness. He rendered me to silence. Something told me to listen to what he had to say, for I myself at the time could not see his implication.

"A magician?" I said meekly, trying to remember a vague memory that would not or could not come. I abandoned the effort.

"No," I answered softly, thinking about where he was going with this. However, once the word was pronounced, there was no going back. I unconsciously understood what I sensed he was saying. I was no magician, but I wanted to be—a spiritual magician, a shaman, a healer. He planted—actually reinforced a seed that was planted long ago before my present birth.

A few months later, the seed had taken roots and deliciously held my imagination and mind. So, it was as I graded the French Regents exams that late June of 2011. Smiling profusely I was, for I was deeply caught in a reverie—age-old questions deliciously appeared before my mind's eye.

"When did the Whole or God 'split' itself? I knew that it is a static perception of sorts and that this experience benefits everyone, but..."

My smile widened as my colleagues spoke and I punched numbers on the $1 calculator that I borrowed from a science colleague.

"*When did the illusion of the split began?*"

"Did she pass?" my foreign language teacher-colleague asked.

My heart was extremely at peace.

There is no such thing as invisibility. It's a matter of reading frequencies. I thought about the night I exited my physical vehicle and stood to the right of the dark entity, observing my body. The inter-dimensional entity was scratching his head, confused and wondering why it could not possess me as it once did. I was just a few feet from this entity, but yet it could not detect my presence. It could not because my ultimate Light Self shielded itself from sight. I thought about perception and how everything is about awareness. The darker an entity, the less aware it is—hence ultimate light power is able to will anything, for Love or the Most Light is the ultimate power.

In terms of my burning intents, I also posed other questions. For instance, I wanted to know what other endeavors Infinity had taken on before this so-called "separation." Did Infinity have prior experiences that were not so physical in nature? I wanted to know how vegetables and other entities such as rocks feel. The last thing I wanted to know came to me while grading the French Regents exams in the lower level of the library at the high school. I was again thinking about the night the inter-dimensional entity attacked me. I remember a scene from the Harry Potter film Deathly Hallows: Part 1. In this scene, Hermione was walking alone in the woods. A few bad guys were also walking in her vicinity. Hermione and these guys existed in the same time-space continuum. If I remember correctly, one was a few seconds in the future while the other a few seconds behind. It was amazing; they could not see her, though they were looking right at her. It was some sort of invisibility cloak—magic.

My colleague's talking momentarily interrupted my visual thoughts.

"Did she pass?" she asked again.

I looked at her for a fraction of a second, then I smiled. A delicious intuition dawned on me.

It's not magic. These movies are not fantasy. They are real. I did what Hermione did in none-physical form. If it could be done in none-physical form, then why couldn't it be done in physical form? Beautiful bastards! These big time writers, scientists, and film directors know something about the true nature of our existence.

They are hiding these so-called secrets in the open—in movies, science fiction novels. They merely label them fiction and have the general population believe that it is make-believe. *Shame on you!* I had them! My spiritual experiences opened up my mind, and once a door is creaked open slightly and the beauty of the Light shines brightly with throbbing desire from the observer, the rest of the door must be opened all the way for the entire luminosity of the Light to take its sensuous beautiful course. I asked myself how I was going to access this source of knowledge. Suddenly, I realized I knew I wanted to be a spiritual magician, and I thought about the Haitian man's pronouncement. Then the visual of the dark entity changing from a physical human being to an intangible being came to me sharply.

From solid to fluidity, none physical!

A wave of calm feeling swept through my heart.

Amazing! The world is not really physical. It is really a static perception.

And humanity is keeping itself prisoner by doggedly subscribing to this tiny, minute aspect of viewing Infinity. It is one thing to merely think these things possible to actually experience them.

Today is the fourth of July—Independence Day. How auspicious—Independence and freedom! Tomorrow I will go to Iquitos, Peru to be healed and to find the answers to my universal questions. The anticipation is great. I am listening to "Set Fire to the Rain," Adele 21 as I write. I am in love with her.

In any case, I have never been to the Amazon rainforest. This is the first time that I will purposely take a natural drug that is not an over-the-counter medication. My expectations are high. This will be one step closer from escaping from the Third Dimension. Once upon a time, my goal was to get rid of the palpitations in my body, and that goal still stands; but because emotions run deep, the desire to see my brother Essevi again is much stronger. He passed in 1993. This was nearly 18 years ago. Much time has passed since I have not conversed with him.

I am sorry I was not able to prevent your death.

"One died. Only one remains," the Togolese plant healer had declared.

I immediately thought of you. You were the only deeply significant soul in my life. No other passing has affected me so deeply. To each his destiny. Not all desires and experiences are the same. You get what you need to advance, not necessarily what you want.

Essevi, do you remember me? Much time has elapsed. Do you recall the Ghanaian guy? The insects we ate together? So close, but yet so far. Thank you for your visit today. Do you remember our brief time in the United States of America?

"One died, one remains!" I said out loud. *What is the nature of soul mates?* We're all soul mates. The most important of my spiritual experiences is not that I survived, it is the fact that you were there for me, though I was not physically aware of it. I love you and will always love you. Peace!

July 5, 2011

I boarded the bus to New York City a while ago. The time is now 4:23 p.m. Somehow I knew that I was going on a trip that would forever change my life for the better. Trees, very green, serenade my eyes. I am fascinated by the physicality of existence. Here we "human beings" *are* so intent at perceiving this physical world as the only way to exist. Somewhere within the space I was sitting in was an intangible being having a none-physical experience—in a none-solid body. We human beings are aware of so little. This trip is the voyage for which I have been waiting.

My mind has been working at the speed of light. While driving today to Kohl's, I recalled the vision that I had in August of 2010, but did not talk about. Something made sense as I recalled the vision. It is all making sense to me now. The August vision took place in a farm in Africa. I could not be sure of the date, but it was clear to me that it was at least many, many years into the future. In this vision, someone was sent after me via Black Magic. As the person approached to attack me, I just changed the scene. I was literally still within the same time space dimension but he did not have access to me.

In any case, going back to what I experienced earlier today, I realized that even in the vision that I just described, I could have used my bodily weapons to defend myself, but I chose a different path—none-violence. I wondered if I will always be able to do that. There are pros and cons of humanity knowing that its soul is a weapon system of light. The powers are mind-boggling.

Perhaps humanity should not know this. The potential misuse is fantastic. I am convinced that in Universal History, there has been such misuse. Yet, in my first book I mentioned it.

Well, I guess…well, I could go back and edit a few things out since the first book is technically not published yet…hum, isn't that in some measure the same thing that has been done to humanity across the millennia? Well, I will take comfort in the thought that most of humanity will not believe me nor will they know how to access this power.

About thirty-five minutes into the bus ride, my mind wandered back to another former important question—

reincarnation. I was suspicious of it. It did not make sense to me—to be stuck in a cycle for hundreds and perhaps thousands of years while using only a fraction of our potential seems odd. I know that free will is always a given, so why the repetition? Reader, if you know something about reincarnation, you must admit that there is something a little off here about this whole process. Sure, some of you may say that the process must be repeated until all the lessons are learned, but I beg to differ. Let me pose you a question: Why the total forgetfulness of our past memories? Yeah, yeah, I know that some of you may still be saying that having access to all of the past memories could be a distraction, and I agree for the most part; but, I sense a bit of manipulation from another frequency. For the love of God, the vast majority of humanity has absolutely no recollection of its previous incarnations. Absolutely none! Just a little! Why not have just a little? Perhaps, we knew that this would be a part of the game, but I still smell trickery here and I intend to explore it, for it is now part of my plan to escape from the Third Dimension. I understand that perhaps, just perhaps multi-dimensional entities were part of if not behind this manipulation—slowing down our spiritual progress, sucking our energy. I was thinking that this could be possible because of negativity. By this, I mean that some people's souls are darker than others. Keeping this in mind, it is possible to convince or set up a system to keep souls coming back and for them not to remember that they were once Black, White, Japanese, Indian, Hindu, and so forth. The manipulation could be done in many levels. One could appeal to the soul's sense of guilt for something negative he or she did in a previous life time.

CHAPTER 6

AYAHUASCA SPIRITUAL HEALING

Wednesday, July 6, 2011:

It was currently 8:20 a.m. Peruvian time. The flight from JFK to Lima was successful. Actually, it was much better than I expected. If you have travelled abroad internationally in recent years or even domestically, you will notice that the airlines have become very stingy with feeding us passengers. This LAN flight to Peru was different. Not only did they have vegetarian food ready at hand for all passengers, they even offered us wine—red and white; and it was free. What was even more astonishing was the fact that I was allowed to have refills.

Presently, I was at my gate 9 waiting for my mother to join me. I walked to the security line. The time was now 8:29 a.m. and I still did not see her, and we were supposed to board at 9:15 a.m. The plane itself was scheduled to take off at 9:50 a.m. for Iquitos, our final destination.

I hope she did not oversleep in her hotel.

Well, I suppose all I can do now is wait and write.

It was about 5:20 p.m. I was with Jose, don Herberto's father. We were at his father's house. His wife went somewhere. I had been writing, killing time. You see, I really don't understand how you could miss your flight and not be aware of the time it takes off especially when you are in a country you have never been before. I called my mother's hotel, whose location I knew only by name. A part of me was hoping that she was running late.

In hindsight, I suppose I should have called her hotel sooner, *but how did she forget about her flight?* Well, I learned that she woke up late. I left instructions for her to board the 6 p.m. flight and to meet me in Iquitos at 8 p.m. I literally had only about ten minutes to decide if I would board, and have her come later. The boarding receptionist was not much help, nor did she care. Nevertheless, I left a note for her to be put into the computer system.

About an hour later, don Herberto and I drove back to the airport in a motorcar to see if my mother would come. The flight arrived late, but it was to my great relief to see her, for I was slightly afraid that she might have returned to the States. But thank God, she made it.

About an hour later, we were on our way to Loreto, where the spiritual center Ashi Meraya is. The cart was going no more than ten miles an hour. The road was muddy, bumpy and rocky. At times, I wondered if we were going to make it to our destination. I had to exit the cart twice. Mud had gotten inside of my shoes. A little over an hour later, we were there.

When we arrived, we were introduced to Bryant and Isabella.

"How was your trip?" she asked.

"It was…what's the word I'm looking for?"

"Tired?" Isabella answered.

"No, the word is relieved."

She kept what seemed to me like a neutral face, but I had to double check.

"Did you come in a motorcar too?"

"Yes."

She posed me a few other questions and we chatted a bit, and I decided to inquire about the object of her journey.

"So, were your expectations met?"

"I got a lot of love, a sense of calm…" she said, moving her hand about to sketch a circle in the air. "There are some intense, scary things at first, then you see wonderful things. You have to experience it for yourself."

She did not really answer my question.

"What I am asking is, good or bad, were your expectations met?"

Bryant answered yes, then came to the dining table where I was. He took a chair, across from me.

"They took a bone out of Bryant's foot," Isabella said.

"A bone that wasn't supposed to be there?"

"Someone put it there," she answered.

I was smiling.

"So, they do this in Canada too?"

"Bad people are everywhere," he answered. I was not convinced he knew much about the use of Black Magic. His answer was a general statement. He lifted his bare right leg to show me.

"I could not walk. I had seen doctors for years and nothing worked."

"Are you saying you think somebody put it there on purpose?" I asked. I sensed he misinterpreted my countenance. "Listen when these things happen, you can be sad about it or laugh. A similar thing was done to me. I have been telling my African friends that white people know Black Magic as well as Blacks, but they don't believe me."

Less than half an hour, we were shown to our quarters. We did not take Ayahuasca the first night. I was able to focus on how the place felt. Each bungalow or casita, or small wooden house had its own bathroom and sink. The shower was cold and there was not any electricity. I had a desk and some candles with which to see at night. Most of the casita walls were empty. That is, they only had screens to keep the mosquitoes out. This allowed for insects, critters, birds, grasshoppers, and the black monkeys to be fully heard throughout the night. There was no way around it—I was in the wilderness, though there were not any wild animals. The place would definitely have had a scary feel to it if I were alone. In about a week, I will be all alone in the sleeping quarters. My mother and Bryant will be gone and the owners and the rest of the family will be across the stream on the other side of the main entrance.

I made a terrible mistake of taking a shower before going to bed. Dead cold—the water was. On top of that, it was cold the entire night. I must say that I was not entirely thrilled about not having electricity in my room or anywhere else in the bungalow compound, but it was good that the mosquito net worked. During the middle of the night, I heard two different insects' noises, but they could not enter.

Morning found me early at about 6 something. My mother and I were in the main dining room by 7 a.m. I wrote for a while intermittently while chatting with her. Somehow or another, Bryant started talking about his foot. My mother was asking most of the questions.

"For four years, this foot was just *like* really messed up."

"Really?" my mother asked.

"So, I tell her," he said, referring to the shaman doña Rcilia, "That was the main thing."

"…you went to doctors?"

"I had scans, surgery, doctors…she sucked out a bone—a fish bone."

He lifted up his right leg again.

"The foot was black. The pain was going all the way to…" he said, pointing to the top of his thigh.

"You should have seen what they put in Isabella's stomach," he said, holding the side of his right stomach.

"What?" I interrupted, "Something was put in her body?"

"Yeah, the shaman took it out."

Then my mother started talking about the things that were put in her body years ago.

"Metal pieces and chains were pulled out of me."

"Chains? You had the whole lot, huh?" Bryant asked with a tinge of a smile.

"She has them on camera—the pictures."

"When they were being taken out, did you see the objects?" Bryant asked.

My mother was standing up. There was a low table between them.

"Yes, she curled a piece of paper toward me, and pulled it out."

"Bryant, did you see the bones that were pulled out of you?"

"Yes."

I was interested because like him, I wanted to know if the bone materialized out of thin air like I had experienced in Togo.

In less than an hour, at 6:30 p.m., the preparation would begin for our first Ayahuasca session. I was extremely calm. I planned to take the strongest dose possible.

Our Ayahuasca experience actually started with a half-hour sauna sweat session. Then, we returned to our respective bungalows to shower. Afterwards, my mother joined me in my room.

"What is that?" she asked rhetorically, "You're drinking red wine before the session?"

"It's just a little."

"You're not supposed to."

"Who's in charge? Moi! It's just a little. It won't do anything."

After drinking a bit of the red wine, I heard something scratching at my door. It was a very friendly and trusting cat that I met earlier that day. I opened the door and let him in. I sat down in a wooden rocking chair, and he walked toward me, asking me with his eyes to pick him up; which I did.

When it was time for us to head to the ceremonial lodge to take our first doze of the Ayahuasca medicine, the cat accompanied us. Maybe I should not even have had the little bit of wine, but oh well.

Don Herberto gave me a glass and a half of the medicine.

People who have drunk Ayahuasca talk about how disgusting it is, but it was not at all for me. I am sure it was not because the dose was weaker. I lied down flat on my back with my eyes closed. Supposedly, bad visions came first before the positive ones.

For the most part, this did not happen. The two times I found myself in a place of total darkness, I was calm, for my previous experiences told me that everything is always alright in the end. For the first ten minutes, I sat against the back wall in a meditation position with my eyes closed. When no visions came to me, I lied down to sleep. I felt a bit nauseous, but I could not vomit.

Sometime later, I sat up and positioned my body erect. I was in a meditating position. My Light Self centered above my head as I sat down against the wall, my legs crisscrossed. As I looked to my right, I was aware that it was my spirit head that was doing the looking. I wanted to see if my mother was alright. I turned back to doña Rcilia who was in front of me. She was doing some sort of prayer. I observed her carefully.

"Why is she trying so hard? I am alright."

I turned my head to my mother again. As I did so, a huge, massive solid less snake stood by my head area. I did not sense any danger, so I left it alone. This must have been the anaconda everybody talks about. After the shaman finished her chanting, I lied back to sleep.

The next part of the vision was completely new to me. Somehow, my mother was by the post office, which was not too far from where I had seen the various colorful lights by the gas station. I, however, was some distance off, looking at her. Then I felt my soul talking to me none verbally.

You know she doesn't understand. She takes it as fear. Try another way. She has not had your experiences.

I immediately understood this as making reference to death of the physical body. Like most people, a part of her still fears death. The message was clear. It does not matter how people perceive the message. Disagreements are futile in the end. There is no judgment.

So cold, I need a blanket for my feet.

Colors started coming—so colorful, but not as intense as in my visions from 2007-2010. My mind was filled with so many questions, *too* many questions. Purple, red, and blue!

Words are not always necessary.

Despite the deluge of questions in my mind, there finally seemed to be a focus:

Let me understand more about who I am.

Pictures of women and men, and objects became concrete to represent God—the *Me* who was conversing with my Mind. However, every time I tried to focus on any one element as representing God, the visual element fades away as a false illusion. This kept happening over and over for several minutes. Then, a colorful dream appeared as a series of images, and finally ending up at the same gas station. The space and air of the gas station were filled with various colors. Then, I found myself in a jungle or woods. I saw myself walking down a narrow pathway with a group of people. I turned and opened my eyes slightly. Darkness swooped across my face. I quickly closed my eyes again.

A few minutes later, I was back in a colorful dream of illusions called the physical world. I was several meters from the gas station again. I went across the street to the left. I saw and chatted with people, while at times I just watched, automatically understanding their state of illusion through invisible vibes of energy and intuition. They were caught in a deep state of static perception that the physical world as they were seeing it would continue in a permanent state of solidity. Then I was aware that people who I was coming across in my waking world were not understanding me when I shared my God message with them. I understood that even my mother was grappling with this. Then suddenly, in this vivid and calm ambiance, a wave of understanding swooped through me.

It doesn't matter!

The message was not oral; it was intuitive. It was clear to me that the intuitive understanding was from my soul. My mind understood that *it really doesn't matter whether or not people disagree, understood or accepted the message.* Then, a thought occurred to me: *Everything is always ok in the end. There is no judgment.* Not even my soul judges its *mind.* It intuitively let me know that there is no superiority between the two—only one is more aware. Then, a wave of intuitive knowing swept through me:

You talk too much. Why do you try so hard?

At the conclusion of the first Ayahuasca session, we struggled with our basic motor skills. Walking became a challenge. Identifying the structure of the wooden house was a major task. I took awkward steps in the near-darkness. A flashlight was shone for me to locate the wooden rail to grab onto.

"Your shoes are here?"

"No, they're, ohm, a little down here."

Those words took great effort to utter. It was actual work uttering them, and as soon as I said them, I felt disconnected to them. Finally, I reached my stringless black shoes. I sat down on the edge of the short wooden stairs. The orange cat appeared out of nowhere, and came directly toward me. Still in a strong daze, and a major disconnection with my mind, I took a momentary break to caress the top of my friend's head. My mother was in front of me. I had both of my hands on her shoulders, and she led the way back. I observed the cat who stopped several times to look into the woods, like a jaguar, like a guardian. Somehow or another, we made it safe and sound to the wooden bungalows.

At about 10:30 a.m. the ensuing day, doña Rcilia convened a post Ayahuasca meeting with us participants. I cannot say that I got much out of it. I related the colors and the déjà-vu vision that I had to them. I even went into the God element of the vision. It was obvious to me that Rcilia and her assistants were not understanding the message, so I refocused the topic to the palpitations in my body. I asked doña Rcilia what she saw when she was praying for me. She said that there is "el humo" within my body.

"A shadow, a smoke? What does that mean?" I asked in Spanish.

"It's something that's alive."

"Alive? How? In what sense?"

I felt myself asking questions after questions, not getting any concrete answers. Given that I did not want to put my idea of what I thought it was into their minds, I stopped.

My mother's review session was the most interesting. She spoke about treasures, being high royalty and queens across several centuries and continents. I do not want to say too much here since it is her story, but I found it interesting that she had a neck problem in her previous life. She also had a chance to talk to her deceased husband—my father. This was interesting, for I did not.

"The incident was bewitched," Rcilia said with serious calm, "It is the envy of others. They think your life is good and are jealous."

After the discussion of the first Ayahuasca session, we went back to our casitas. Presently, we were in my bungalow. I looked at my mother, and brooded. Here was a woman who had to worry about not having enough clothes to wear, or enough food to eat for years and years in Togo, West Africa.

"When I was pregnant with your little brother, I did not know where the next day's food was going to come from to feed you guys."

But, she was once grand—queens and rulers of great civilizations. To me, that is the beauty of being God. You are everything and nothing. You can be a small thing or a big thing. It does not mean you're worth less or more, for everything matters. No matter how insignificant the tiniest insects or the smallest thing seems, there is no hierarchy between anything. The insect is not worth less than you simply because you're human or because you have a voice apparatus or because you are bigger. To me, it is absolutely beautiful that you can be reduced to simplicity and hardship if that is what is needed for you to reach the Light, to reduce the false ego. Impose a hierarchy between you and other things, and you will put yourself in a state of false illusion.

Friday, July 8, 2011:

Doña Rcilia gave us a cold Ayahuasca leaf bath by the stream by our casitas. My mother went first. I followed. Rcilia started by smoking a mapacho (i.e., organic tobacco) bit by bit and then blowing the smoke into my body. Don Alfredo assisted. When she was halfway through the tobacco, she stopped and observed the shape of the ash. The top was curved.

"Your body is bad," she said, looking at me with an immobile gaze.

I immediately thought this was due to the things in my body. I was right, and she concurred. The bath water was very cold. I held my breath the whole time.

We started the second Ayahuasca ceremony session at about 8:15 p.m. Herberto offered me a dose of the medicine. I was prepared for the session this time, hoping to get rid of the palpitations in my body. I focused my mind on where I wanted the healing. It seemed as if I had been there for hours, when in actuality I was probably there for only one hour. No particular vision came to me, only darkness. It was a constant flow of images of darkness. I was able to decipher objects, colors within this flow. That was it. Nothing more! Unlike the previous night, I was only slightly tipsy. I kept telling them that the medicine was not strong enough, but they wanted to follow what they had planned.

I took my hand off my chin, and lowered my head. I was staring into the void, pondering, trying to find that happy place when I heard a voice to my right.

"Concentrate Agbe!" I heard don Herberto say in Spanish.

This is the second night that everybody else was successful at vomiting and I had not.

After the ceremony, we went back to our casitas. That was when the weirdest thing happened. It was really freaky, and it felt like I was in a spiritual world. This was the type of things that I only heard about in Africa. I mean, here I was in my room hearing the weirdest of incantations. It was a continuous chant, a charm. I was sitting in my quasi-dark room, trying to figure out where the magical chanting was coming from.

"Dada, is that you chanting? Dada?"

She did not say anything for a while, then said:

"No talking, I'm dizzy. Tomorrow."

I reached for the match in the near total dark room. I tried lighting several matches, but no cigar. The luring chanting persisted. It seemed like it was coming from above the little wooden houses. This was the same chant as the first night. This time it seemed more pronounced. I had to get to the bottom of this. I exited my room and sat outside in the woods in a wooden chair, looking to my left. The moonlight shone, illuminating the grey sand covering the narrow pathway to my left. I stared at the pathway pondering the spirituality of the place. The loud, but soft chanting from above the trees continued. It was persistent. I tried to decipher where it was coming from. It was definitely not the birds or the insects, for they too were making their own noise. I leaned forward in my chair. I was alone in the semi-twilight. Suddenly, an odd energy swooped around my right ear. I shook it off with my right hand.

I think it's time to go back to my room. Who knows what kinds of bad spirits are out here!

As soon as I went back inside the house, a loud noise could be heard from outside. It sounded like a rooster, but not. It seemed too powerful to be a rooster. And besides, *what in the world would a rooster be crowing in the middle of the night?*

It was definitely not much past 1 a.m. in the morning. *How awesome!* The rain was coming down hard. The sound was musical, delightful.

I got into bed. The spellbound chant of the spirit of the jungle persisted. This was all too unusual. It was something out of a movie, make-believe magic. If I had not had my surreal spiritual experiences in the last few years, I might have doubted my ears.

In the afternoon, we gathered around to have a discussion about the previous night's Ayahuasca session. Bryant said something disturbing.

"I felt a bad energy around my stomach area, as if something was trying to get inside me."

I raised my eyebrows in concern.

"It didn't get in!" doña Rcilia said.

"Your icaro was protecting you."

Bryant's animal protector was a big wolf, which he described as he saw it in his Ayahuasca vision.

I have seen enough in my life to know that these things are real. I am looking forward to leaving. Two weeks is a long time. But, I don't really want to leave.

The conflict in my *feelings* was most interesting to my mind.

A couple of days later:

A few days have passed and much has transpired. I was losing hope that the negative energy in my body was never going to come out. As the days passed, I started to make up reasons why I should leave early. Such reasons included but not limited to: (1) the room can get sometimes cold at night, (2) I have been bitten by mosquitos, (3) the bed is uncomfortable, (4) I am starving myself by waiting 20 hours between lunch and breakfast the ensuing day, and (5) my last vision may have been right that the people here were going to kidnap me. I knew this last reason was completely absurd because as soon as I thought about it, I was smiling. It was the things inside.

Although these thoughts occupied my mind, I did not give in. I had to keep going somehow. I partook in spiritual ritual purifications and mud baths. Despite these healing activities, every once in a while I would revisit the reasons for departing early. Such was the state of my mind when I went in for my third Ayahuasca session with the two shamans at about 8 p.m. They made the brew stronger, and this time gave me two and a half doses of the medicine. I prayed over it and quickly swallowed it. This time, it tasted nasty. Twenty or so minutes passed in the darkness, and nothing happened. I twisted and turned around in my plastic mat. Suddenly, I was back in the dark entities' subconscious world again. As before, everything spun around in circular motions of diametrical pictures and shapes in mostly dark images. I was aware that I was not afraid of the darkness—hence evil, for it was merely fear. That was all I had. I sensed that don Herberto was watching me, though I could not see him. Just as I guessed it, he was.

"Sit up Agbe," he said.

He said some prayers over me as he blew his tobacco smoke over my head.

"Never have I seen anyone so strong."

By strength, he meant my resilience to pain. He then walked over to my mother. I kept my ears to her to make sure she was alright. At one point I jerked up when I heard her vomiting suddenly and violently.

Don Herberto spoke in Spanish and I translated for my mother. He wanted to know if it were alright with my mother to add another dose given that she was leaving in two days. My mother and I both agreed. After giving the dose to her, he came to me. I sensed that the moment was extremely important, so I cleared my mind and focused. I prayed over the Ayahuasca before drinking it. I focused on getting rid of whatever was in my body. This particular dose was quite nasty. Don Herberto began to suck around my forehead. I kept my concentration on what I wanted. Soon, he left and I lied down. Bits and pieces of the same dark vision kept coming back to me. The recurring theme of being in a trance state also kept appearing. This made me question the intentions of my two shamans. I was confused. Rcilia and Herberto's repetitive chants were the same as in the visions I had before coming to the rainforest. In those visions, we attended a ceremony whose end I was not able to see. All around me were repeating light colors. Somehow, I was made to think that this was a bad thing—that I was being duped. I did not know how or why, but it reminded me of the current state of humanity, under a deep hypnotic sleep state.

I lied down on the mat on my side, and then on my stomach. Then, the real manipulation began. Don Herberto was chanting the Shipibo shamanic spell louder and louder to help us reach the desired state of sub-consciousness. I saw myself in the darkness again. This time, it was a little different. Among the constantly rotating and turning dark colors, in which I was moving around in circular space, there were small black ants under the images. As I rotated across, I had the distinctive impression that I was being covered by the ants. I realized that I was not afraid. I had overcome the shadow and the darkness. My logical mind pondered this subliminal subconscious message.

It was a representation of death.

Maggots and other insects eat the human body once it is dead. It was absolutely clear to me that these dark forces in me were trying to fool my subconscious to be afraid. This was utter insanity, for they should have realized that I was no longer afraid of death given the fact that they had been in my body for a very long time.

The next piece of trickery came in the form of the manipulation of my body energy. My upper chest area took heat. I was so, so confused, yet I was calm. An image of ShopRite flashed before my mind's eye, and I remembered being in this similar predicament before. At that time the New York psychics Lisa and Linda insisted that I bring them about ten thousand dollars to help me take away the witchcraft spells that were casted on me. My mind drifted to the present.

"I might as well go back to my room," I heard myself say aloud with despair. I was frustrated that these things were still in my body. Perhaps I thought that simply taking the medicine and not vomiting would suffice to cast away these dark things. I turned to sleep until it was time to go.

Don Herberto came to me and instructed me to reach out both of my hands, and then to join them. He placed a rock in them. He said some chants, and I focused really hard on the rock. I imagined the things in my body seeping to the rock. He blew more tobacco smoke on the center of my head.

Despite his best effort, the vomit would not come. Then he began to explain to me what he saw my soul doing.

"You're neutralizing the negativity…You've done this for a very long time."

I immediately understood this as "keeping the balance between the negative and positive forces in me."

"For your protection, your icaro will be Mother Ayahuasca," he said, utterly shocking and rendering me speechless.

Mother Ayahuasca? Can't be! This is a huge, very busy positive force in the world. I felt so loved, for this was the highest of all protection anyone could get. My state of tranquility was augmented instantly.

The ceremony ended a minute or two later, and don Herberto began speaking, basically repeating the same thing he said in private.

"This is the first time I have had to use this rock. Never in all my years have I seen a soul so strong."

"With all the negativities, right?" I said.

I got up to obtain my chacruna medicine.

What happened next baffled my imagination so deeply that I would never see myself the same way again. We were on our feet, ready to leave, and Don Herberto was talking about the fact that it was Mother Ayahuasca who had chosen me. For the life of me, I did not know what he said next, but it rendered me to laughter, for it was really funny. I had a delicious thought about love.

Is it enough?...It's always enough.

The interesting thing here was that I absolutely knew that I had many, many dark entities in my body. Upon having this thought, I immediately sensed their happiness. *I made them happy. For a brief second they lost control of their fear, and remembered the beauty of their Infinity.*

Quickly now, I saw myself advancing toward the spit spot. I vomited like I had never vomited before. Every push was very, very physical. Forget the film The Exorcist or the like that you might see in movies or television. This was unbelievably intense. One needed to have put a camcorder in my head to have been able to understand what I was experiencing. There were so many of them in my throat, mouth, and head. They seized whatever part of the inside of my head they could to stay in my body. Their screams were demonic. A lot of dark, red, and tiny glimmers of white light flashed in my head. They fought hard as if their existence depended on it. Some fought physically hard against exiting my throat. Others dug their spiritual, dimly-solid dark fingers into my skull. Vomit after vomit rendered their struggle futile. I felt like my skull was being pulled asunder. Still, I pressed on until I seemed to have run out of liquid in my body. Tears streamed down my cheek. After I stopped vomiting, I stared into my bowl. It was full of liquid. In the center was a dark stick-like figure. It had two legs and a center that formed the spine. There was no head, and if there were, I was not able to see it because the moonlight did not illuminate the spot enough. I stayed on all fours—stupefied and sweating. Tears flowed from my face to the floor. I raised myself up, still on my knees, and wiped my face. That was an incredible experience. The demons screamed in my head as if I were sending them to their deaths. What was even more astonishing was their physical manifestation within me. This was definitely something out of a Hollywood movie, but worse: with more intensity.

On our regular path back to the casitas, don Herberto posed me a question:

"Do you know why Mother Ayahuasca chose to be your protector?"

My head was dizzy, my movements clumsy, but I managed to muster something somewhat intelligent.

"Because of all the dangers in the future: in Africa, in America."

"Good, now you understand the vision that you had: why you were suspicious."

I thought this was interesting considering that I did not mention anything about it to him.

"Yeah, they were trying to stop me from coming here to get the healing."

I turned to look at him. He nodded in agreement.

By the time we returned to our casitas, it was about 1:30 a.m. The moonlight graced the trees, plants and the grey, beach-like sand in our pathway. I was ecstatic. No! I felt loved by Mother Ayahuasca, the spirit of the Amazon. I went into the shower as soon as I went into my room. I scrubbed and scrubbed my body with my African sponge, as if I were getting rid of the negative energy in my system. That was the best cold shower I had honestly *ever* taken. My heart was tranquil. I was in bed now, thinking about Mother Ayahuasca, and my brother Essevi.

Is it enough?...Is a smile or a sudden moment of happy thought ever enough? Yes, love is always enough.

Insects buzzed very loudly like a smooth melody. Suddenly, a loud fire-cracker-like noise sounded in the sky.

"Hey Agbe!" Bryant called out form his casita across the other side of the woods, "Happy birthday."

I smiled and said thank you. My mother, who was in the other casita to the right of me pronounced firmly:

"He was not born yet. What time is it?"

"It a little past 1:30 a.m. Togo is about six hours ahead of us."

"You're not born yet."

"But I thought you said that I was born at 6:45 or 46?"

"No, 10 o'clock."

I heard the melodious chanting of Mother Ayahuasca. However, this time, her voice could literally be heard near my pillow. She was letting me know that she was there to protect me. Thoughts of my brother always fighting for me came to me again, and I suddenly said out loud:

"Nice job Essevi," which was followed by giving him a right thumb up. I immediately saw and felt his presence and joy next to the right of me in the bed.

I tried to sleep. It was futile. I was only able to sleep for about an hour that night because I was overcome with so much joy. This was fine, for it gave me the opportunity to reflect on the experience I just had. I thought about the fact that I had been too harsh on my Light Self. My mind was not aware that it was busy trying to keep us all alive. If Ello[2] had not "hidden away," the demonic entities might have overpowered me. The reason for this is now clear. My mind was not aware that the soul existed. Therefore, it assumed that it was the only force in the body there is. The soul needed the mind to wake up and to understand that it too cannot die—only transform from one source of energy to another. Once slightly awakened, then the soul could direct it more efficiently. An excellent driver (i.e., the soul) cannot drive a none-functioning car.

I closed my eyes to sleep. I do not think I slept for more than an hour and a half before I woke up. I decided to ponder my recent past. So much was now clear to me. The reason why food such as okra and yams excited the pain in my stomach was not because I was allergic to these types of food, but because the negative entities enjoyed them.

[2] This is a genderless third person singular Spanish pronoun.

Hence, whenever I ate okra they rushed to where it lands in my stomach and feasted. The pain came from the deluge or the concentration of their negative energy in one place.

I felt their physical presence within my entire head when I was trying to vomit them out. Maybe they had to take a more solid form within me because otherwise they could not "stick" to me. This awareness that they were physically inside of me would compel me to find any means possible to vomit them out.

I turned to the left wall of my bed. An image of my Caucasian doctor came to mind. I was at the hospital in Rockland County. The medical doctor and I were talking about a cold that I had. This was sometime in April or May of 2009. He was debating whether or not to give me a prescription.

"Listen, I'll take the prescription."

"You just have a cough," he said half-jokingly, "Wait a few days to see if you get better before taking it. Take no more than one a day."

I left his office and went home. I found myself near Lehman College a few days later underneath the train station. I was on the telephone talking to Lisa, the psychic.

"My chest is really bad, Lisa."

"Your brother kept saying: My brother is going to be fine."

Neither Lisa nor the doctor knew the real battle that was going on inside me. I brought my mind back to the Peruvian jungle. I turned in my bed. The insects and the birds were still singing.

When can I expect day break in this Amazon jungle? I can't sleep.

I lied flat on my stomach, waiting for sleep to come. When it did not, I started thinking again about the medicine that the doctor gave me. This time, I found myself on the third floor of my house. I defied the doctors and took two pills instead of one.

They don't always know what they are talking about.

The next day, my weak, drained chest began to regain its strength.

I must sleep! Tomorrow is going to be a big Ayahuasca battle.

The ensuing day:

For most of the next day, I maintained my positive feeling. Nothing could touch me. I was cracking jokes and laughing as if the present was all there was. But, I supposed I could not maintain this high feeling until the battle was complete. Little did I know that this night was going to be the "worse" one yet.

Bryant was the first to vomit. My mother followed. Try as I might, I felt no nausea whatsoever.

About an hour and a half later, Don Herberto gave me half a dosage of his own stronger Ayahuasca medicine. Then he placed the same rock as the previous day in the palm of my hand. I concentrated on it a bit, and then he had me take it to my heart area near the left breast close to my gorge. I lied down, trying to resist the all-consuming negative, suffocating feeling that was working in my chest area into my throat. He had me hold down the small grey rock on the ground. After a while, I realized that there was no way in hell the demons in me were going to let me vomit voluntarily. So, I leaned forward and tried to vomit. My first two attempts were futile. Then, I had an idea—why not put my fingers to both sides of the temples of my head and summon the energy that way.

Eureka!

There were literal screams inside my head. As before, colors flashed in head, but this time, they were much darker than the others. Though I was aware of many entities refusing to exit, there was one in particular that screamed out like a demon. It was like a stubborn, spoiled-rotten child refusing to do what he or she knows must be eventually done to recover his or her own bright positive light.

Quickly now, I summoned the force within me to expel them. That particular demon grabbed onto the sides of my throat. When success was almost mine, it dried my throat.

Water! So dry! Water!

I let go of the struggle in order to reason with him. I told him that I did not hate him, and that everything would be alright. I asked him to think about how much pain he was in because he refused to accept love. All of my supplications were in vain. The fear in him was too deep. I really did not know how any being could survive like that.

So much suffering! Try again Agbessi. Tomorrow is another day. No, there is no tomorrow! The battle is now!

Doña Rcilia came to help me. She was talking about how much I had vomited, and later would point out to me that I had done well. I, apparently, had vomited a lot of dark liquid, and even quite a few worms.

Don Herberto vomited tremendously that night. I had heard a lot of noise coming from his direction. Apparently, he had sucked too many demons into himself, and had to release them before he became really sick.

Night of July 12, 2011:

We left our casitas at about 8:45 p.m. My jaguar cat came to accompany us. He always seemed to know when I needed him most. He went around my legs and I stroke his head with my right hand. He stopped to look into the woods every few minutes like a soldier protecting his family or unit.

Before the session began, I was most delighted to hear don Herbert's words of tranquility.

"No hatred, no dislike! Put yourselves in a place of love. That's when Ayahuasca works best."

I translated this into English for Bryant, and then thought about my own decision to pursue the love solution. He and I were on the same page. I closed my eyes and began asking for help.

"Essevi, Mother Ayahuasca, and soul of mine, it's time. Help me muster up the strength to do this. Essevi, give me a smile when I need it most."

"Quieres tomar un vaso y medio?" Herberto asked me.

"No, I was thinking two. The battle is on."

"He's a champignon!" don Herberto's uncle don Alfredo cheered on.

I sat down, meditated and awaited my medicine. The shamans were still chanting—things were taking too long.

No haste Agbessi.

I went to my knees to receive the medicine. I held the small shot glass between both of my fingertips, and prayed over it again. Then I swallowed the sewage-like brew as quickly as I could. I took another. I lied back in my usual sitting position against the wall with my eyes closed—waiting for the medicine to kick in. After about twenty minutes, I knew it was going to be a long night. Though my stomach was uncomfortable, I felt no desire to throw up. I lied down for a while and thought about the strategy that I devised during the day. I put myself on all fours like a bull, a beast, an animal. I focused on all the palpitations and discomfort and brought them to my stomach. I strained every part of my body—the motion going from my toes to my legs, arms, then from the top of my head to my throat. Finally, I launched a vomit which seized at my throat. I did it again as I held onto this second "knot" in my stomach. Finally, on the third try, I was able to vomit a few drops. Then, as if I were dreaming, I saw a being, a red demon, returning to its throne. It had followers. There was more, but I cannot recall the rest. It was as if something was blocking my recollection. It did not matter, for I myself found it difficult to accept. It was something out of a movie. This was too much for even me. Then I lost my neutral stance. I began to feel their dark, extremely negative world more deeply. I found myself thinking:

If this is evil, then I don't want to know.

For the time being, I did not want to know the origin of evil or negativity. It was too much. I was not ready for it.

How do they survive all this negativity? No wonder they are always messing with our world.

Theirs is ugly. There is no other word for what I felt. It was pure ravaging, yucky-ugly, raw negativity that drains one's bright light. To them, our world must seem heavenly. No amount of power or money or control could ever convince me to live in their world even for five minutes. It was at that exact moment that I thought maybe my time would be better served by exploring positivity. I had enough of the taste of negativity. Well, at least for now. I must admit that there is a lingering desire in me to find the answers to the questions to which I originally posed before embarking on this journey to South America. A part of me still wanted to know the origin of the "separation" of Infinity and when negativity or evil began. I still wanted to know how reincarnation is being manipulated after death of the physical body. But, I suppose you don't always get what you want, but rather what you need.

I do have a feeling that I just may come back to these questions later. For now, I will build up my spiritual light energy, regain some of my lost stamina, and continue the journey later with my shaman apprenticeship. This too I am a little weary about. You know, this whole business of sucking in other people's negative energy to heal them just has not settled in with me yet. Right now, I do not see myself doing that.

For what seemed to be days, but in actuality probably an hour or so, I tried to convince the demons that love is the best solution. I decided to try something new. I sat up on my buttocks and crossed my legs, and leaned my back against the wooden wall. I reached inside my chest with both hands. I laid my right hand against my left chest near the center of my throat, while placing the left on my lower stomach. A monologue ensued.

"You're in me. Can't you feel the suffering? So much unnecessary suffering! Don't you care that you're hurting yourself?"

I waited for a few seconds, and then I went down to vomit again. Again, I mustered up all of my bodily energy. I hurled out empty, dried air again. I wanted to give up, then thoughts of encouragements came to me loud and clear.

Agbessi, you can't stop now. They think they are stronger than you. Yet, it was you who carried them for years.

Despite the discomfort, I started to believe.

"*There is a love that cannot falter: you! No matter how many souls you have killed or civilizations you have destroyed, there is no punishment. The rest of Infinity will welcome you back. God cannot destroy Itself. It's an impossibility! Do you remember that morning on the*

Tappan Zee Bridge? Do you remember me sensing your overwhelming feeling of never being able to reach the rest of Infinity?"

I pressed my hands on my chest and stomach.

"*Help me help you.*"

I lied on my stomach to begin the next part of the battle.

"Show me a time when you were beautiful. Please show me."

My answer came in waves of flowing, moving dark colors and weightless, but fluid energy. The negativity began to intensify. I felt it even more strongly. Then, I remembered the time I felt happy.

"*Is it enough? Even a slight, tiny glimmer of Light?...Stop! Stop giving me more of your darkness. I asked you to show me a time when you were beautiful. There is still a tiny spark of beauty in you. MUSTER IT UP!*"

By the grace of God, a miracle had been performed. The dark leaf to my right started changing color to a shade of green.

Yeah, I thought so. That will be enough for today.

I took a break. Doña Rcilia came to pray for me. She was singing the most beautiful Shipibo Indian melody.

The smile, Agbe!

I sketched a smile on my face and started rocking my head to the tune. This was the same person whose authenticity I had questioned during the first ceremony. She was doing a great job. She left and don Herberto came to take over. I tried to vomit with him too but nothing really came of it. I brought up my right hand, and as if scratching up all the pain in my body, I summoned up everything to my stomach and went on all fours again. The creature rose within my head, shoulders, and back. There, it kept its stubborn firm grip. It felt so physical within my back. Don Herberto was somehow perceiving this. He began sucking the negative energy into him. He chanted and seemed to have been standing over me for a long time. Then, he walked toward his mat. He started throwing up before he took four steps. He vomited like I had never seen before; and I wondered why the intensity.

He sat down to discuss the session with us. We were still in the darkness, not much light. What he said was astounding.

"The shadow is deep. I took some in and had to vomit it out. You saw that right?"

"Yes, I did."

"Sometimes a new strategy is needed. You'll have to find another way of getting it out."

I was stuck. Tonight's strategy was the best I had. I did not know what else I could do to have this thing exit my body. As he spoke, an idea came to my mind—laughter, a smile.

That might work.

"I have an idea, but sometimes, it is best not to let them know."

"Well said."

He paused for a brief second.

"I saw a man with his two-headed snake. They were really vicious. One of the snakes had a monstrous face. The other had a humane face. They launched themselves toward me. I told the man to stop. He was black. Not too tall or too short: five foot seven or eight inches. He was really aggressive. He told me to stop helping you or you're going to have a problem."

"For you to stop helping me or he was going to hurt you?" I clarified.

"Yes," he answered, "One of the snakes launched himself at me. I took out his eyes, the one with the monstrous looking face. The man said that he was sent to watch you."

"In a bad way?"

"Yes, to make sure you never get healed. I told him that this is my world and that he's the visitor."

"Somebody sent this person after me?"

"Yes. I said to myself that Agbe is going to get sick."

I took this to mean the end of me.

"In any case, it's too bad because there is no such thing as death. My physical death means absolutely nothing. As long as I try to accomplish my goals, then I am already successful," I said to him emphatically.

"The shadow is too strong. I see now why Mother Ayahuasca took charge, saying 'I'll watch over Agbe,'" he said.

Don Herberto did not quite understand how these malevolent, dark entities tormented me physically and mentally. He did not know that *that* night when my Light Self exited my physical body a new sense of awareness had dawned on my *mind*—that my perception of these beings had drastically changed. I saw them as weak, lambs pretending to be lions, who were preying on human beings. I had become the lion, and if I had not been given proper direction, only Infinity knows what I would have done to them and their lot, and those people who had casted spells me. This also applied to those in Africa who had slaughtered my father in the street of the Ivory Coast. My Light Self quickly understood this and so gave me the infinity message. The Light Self knew what It was capable of. It was then that I made myself the none-verbal promise not to ever, ever let anything hurt any part of me that deeply again. An interior battle had begun—against the darkest part of myself that accepted the most beautiful part of himself. It is that part that refused depression no matter how many demons entered my body. It is that part of me that longed for beauty, that was no longer afraid to cry, that felt sorry for the negative entities that sought to destroy me.

Then, a thought occurred to me—none of the suffering had to happen. It happened because there was a hook in me that either allowed it or was unaware of it. Nothing happens by accident. If I had not allowed my consciousness to be pre-occupied by all of my childhood pains as well as taking Black Magic seriously, then these negative beings would not have had a chance. I was distracted, distracted by low vibrational energy.

How long have I been distracted? Energy goes where concentration is. It is unbiased, like the law of attraction.

I stopped to consider don Herberto's words. I did get sick. I was depressed for years. I just faked it until I made it.

It was only after the pronouncement of his words that I understood why my soul went deep within its physical vehicle—It was trying to survive.

"But I am positive we will come out alright and you will be able to sleep like a baby," don Herberto said.

I thought about who could have sent the snake-man after me. Three names in the village of Kpalimé and Kusuntu came to my mind. I did not understand how the person could hate me so passionately when I did not grow up there. They do not even know me at all.

"This problem must go beyond this current incarnation of our bodies," I said outside of myself.

Don Herberto listened without saying a word, and at the time I had no idea how dead right I was.

"Check out my grandmother to see if she has anything to do with it. There were people behind her."

"Tomorrow, I will ask for the man's name."

"None of this makes any sense. You don't send demonic entities after someone for nothing. There is more to the story."

The conversation now turned to Bryant who had an awesome vision.

"I saw her!"

"Get out of here! You really saw her clearly?"

"Yes! She's beautiful!" he exclaimed.

"That's awesome, man." I was really happy for him. I had my smile back.

"This is for Bryant," Herberto said, "He has good moral character. Normally, we only do diets for two weeks, not one week because it is really difficult. But when you asked me, my first thought was to say no, but then I looked into your eyes and decided to take you in. There are two ways shamans protect their patients. The first entails taking on an object and to pretend that thing is you. The second is when the patient's icaro becomes himself. You are your own protector now."

"That's awesome!" Bryant said after I finished translating.

"There's something that I want you to do for this center of healing. When you go home, spread the word about this place with your family and friends."

"Oh, definitely. I want to thank you both for doing a great job. I want you two to know that I respect a great deal what you do."

"We're now going to give Mr. Chavez his *icaro*, then we're finished."

"Guys, I have to go to the restroom soon or we're going to have an unpleasant accident here," I said.

Bryant laughed boisterously. I did not think that the rest of them understood me. Besides, I did not want to be impolite. I held it in as I stood in the circle with the four of them. Don Herberto prayed for don Alfredo. During the prayer, I started getting a very uncomfortable feeling in my stomach. For the life of me, I cannot recall what was said next, but it made me laugh. We were beginning to walk toward the exit when someone made a joke. Maybe what ensued next was due to Mother Ayahuasca, Essevi and my two shamans' keeping their promise to help. In any case, there are moments when the unexpected happens and you cannot help but wholeheartedly feel and believe in love.

As soon as I took two steps toward the door, I saw myself spinning my other foot toward my vomit bowl, making a 270-degree rotation. I was on all fours again like a wild animal. Voices screeched out. I vomited effortlessly. The demons were trying to resist, but resistance was absolutely futile for most of them. I vomited faster and faster, trying to understand where this force was coming from. Don Herberto came to pray over me. Finally, I felt free. I knew that quite a few of them were thrown out. Tears rolled down my face.

When it was all over, I told everybody to take notice of when I vomited. Then I went to the bathroom to do a number 1. Afterwards, I stood on the wooden ledge, looking at the bushes, the leaves below. I was calm. There was some progress tonight, though not as much as I would have wanted, but I felt alright because I tried hard. That is all I can ever expect of myself. I went back inside. Having taken no more than five or six steps, don Alfredo stopped me.

"Your family was protecting you."

"My brother?"

"They were trying to get back into your body."

"Too bad, my body is shielded. Once you get out, you can't get back in," I answered, but was really thinking: *That's amazing. These entities will never stop.* Their stubbornness cannot be compared to my family's pure love.

They tried so hard. A part of me that night said, *"Maybe they should have let me die. Why try so hard for someone who did not really consider other forms of existence? Someone who reluctantly took on bits of the world belief system?"*

I walked home that night with my yellow cat again. Bryant and I were far behind Herberto and Rcilia. We were both ecstatic. We both spoke that night about being the lucky ones—to know that love is the ultimate power. I, of course, had to add:

"You know as I have said before 'A thousand Superman have absolutely nothing on us.' But, let me revise that. A million Superman have absolutely nothing on us."

I felt I learned a lesson that goes straight to Infinity. There are souls that are so behind that they will require several millennia to reach the same acceptance of knowledge as us. So, I felt I was the lucky one to bask in infinite awareness, reducing the unnecessary suffering and to move on to lighter and lighter forms of consciousness. The battles I have chosen are difficult, but the rewards are immense.

Bryant was laughing again. It was such a delightful, light hearted walk home.

Upon arriving at my casita, I sat outside in a wooden, rocking chair for a few minutes. I was alone, and enjoying the night's success. The word "food" came to my mind in my native Earth language. I understood that I could not even have had a chance at success without having changed my diet to organic food. It was clear to me that once I stopped eating Monsanto's genetically polluted, poisonous food, I began to feel better physically, emotionally, and spiritually. I am sure this reduced the demons' negative energy in my body.

Alone in my room that evening, I also understood that demons, spirits, ghosts, aliens, and inter-dimensional entities are pretty much the same in their base essence. Demons tend to take ugly looking forms, but this does not have to be. Souls are the same, whether they come from lighter or darker dimensions. The real difference is in how much each soul has to advance.

Bryant left two hours later that night, at four o'clock in the morning.

Not much transpired that day. My mother insisted on participating in one more Ayahuasca intake before leaving for the States. As a result, we did not sleep much that night. Twilight found us rushing out of the jungle at about 4:30 a.m. We were late and out of our element. We sat in the back of the motorcar. This one was more like a small wagon.

The bitter suffocating feeling in my chest and throat returned with immensity. I put my hand over the area and observed the road in pain. So plain the road was, but yet so filled with so much spirit. The motorcar rocked and I tightly held onto the metal bar to the left.

The morning air swept through and rendered us to a shivering stillness. My mother took out her cloth and put it around us. Unfortunately, the wind and the constant rocking of the car separated me from the sheet. I took my side and put it around her.

"You don't need it?"

"I'm fine."

We arrived at the airport about an hour and a half later. Presently, we were waiting for the young man behind the baggage check-in counter to resolve my mother's itinerary issue. I did not know what I was thinking, but I said something I immediately knew I should not have.

"I made it to 35." I was smiling, but my mother did not appreciate my happy state of mind. She gave me a knock on the head with her hand.

"That's not nice."

When it was time to go, she gave me a worried look.

"I wish there's something I can do."

"Smile. There's no point in having the two of us suffer." I had my hand to my chest. "I'll be fine. I'm always fine in the end. You have to remember that I chose this. I knew the risks I would encounter, but I chose this life regardless."

I gave her a hug and left.

I did not start feeling better until I returned to the jungle at about 11:30 a.m. I saw doña Rcilia standing by her casita.

"How are you?" she asked.

"I was in pain all day: my chest and throat areas."

"There is only a little left."

"Are you sure?"

"Yes."

I walked away to my casita feeling relieved, but deep inside I did not believe her. Nevertheless, I appreciated her optimism.

I did not take Ayahuasca the ensuing day. I thought it would be best to rest, to let the lessons sink in. I spent much of my time thinking about Mother Ayahuasca and Mother Earth. In terms of Mother Ayahuasca, I was fully aware that she is a very important soul on the planet. She oversees the spiritual well-being of all the plants, trees, and animals that reside in her bosom. As you will recall, I actually came into contact with her as a huge anaconda during my first Ayahuasca session. She can take any form she wishes, just like human beings' souls can.

I also thought about how wonderful Mother Earth is without really remembering why. My mind shifted to a busy street corner in Lomé, the capital city of Togo. I saw myself conversing with my oldest aunt Amélino.

"She's alive," she said, referring to Mother Earth. The "she" in the Ewe language translates better as "ello" in Spanish, a neutral, sexless pronoun. In any case, ever since then I have been pondering if she actually has an actual soul just like you and I. It took about a year and seven months to learn the veracity of this. While sleeping one evening before coming here to the Peruvian Amazon, I saw myself extending just right above a huge surface of the Earth. My soul was extended and I could sense the Earth's essence, though I could not see an actual light body. My uncertainty of the Earth having or not having a soul was mostly gone that day. Like my aunt, I too was now convinced that the Earth has an actual soul. She is fantastic. She is very giving and loving. We live in a sphere of consciousness that is way too dark, negative, but yet she accepts all of us as her soul mates. She chooses to suffer so that all dark souls and not so dark souls can cleanse themselves of their negativity, to have a chance to learn, to reach a state of lighter consciousness. She does all this despite daily suffering. That is impressive. That is unconditional love!

It is because of the unconditional love that I experienced here that I now turn to those of you who have killed a single person or a multitude or even committed murder on a mass scale. It is never too late. You are not forever damned to suffering. No priest, rabbi, pope, president, or holy religious work may stand in your way. You do not need their permission to turn back to the Light. You do not even need permission to exist no matter what you have done. It is called unconditional love. Though it may seem difficult to understand, believe me you, that there are souls out there in the entirety of the universe who have done much worse. The horror and negativity is horrendous to feel. Yet, Infinity wants them back to the Light. Infinity must have them back to the Light. The choice is theirs. The choice is yours. It is never too late to reduce the negativity you are carrying. NEVER! But, the longer you wait, the more difficult it is to cleanse yourself of the literal negative dark energy that covers your soul. The longer you wait, the more you will suffer. So, I ask you to come back to the Light, your own Light. Come back by doing something positive that makes you happy. Come back by repaying in kindness those whom you have hurt. Come back by helping others whom you did not hurt.

Those of you who are already on the path of expanding the Light, thank you. Every soul that advances, benefits us all. God speed!

CHAPTER 7

NEARLY KILLING MY SHAMAN

Morning found me brooding about the culprits who had casted the spells to allow the demons to enter my body. Hawa, her mother Agusta, and her oldest aunt comprise part of the group of culprits.

I clearly recall my mother quoting what Agusta said: "Hawa will only marry Yema's son. If he doesn't, then he will find no one else."

For those of you who did not read my first book and therefore do not know the family, let me briefly explain. Hawa and her family are originally from Kusuntu, a village near Kpalimé in the south of Togo, West Africa. In 2007, I decided to settle down and build a family with someone from "back home." This was a mistake, for immediately upon hearing this, Agusta and her wicked older sister went to sorcerers to cast spells on me to make sure that I would marry her daughter. It was during that time when the palpitations began in my body.

My Trinidadian friend was also part of the gang of culprits. We first met when she asked for help with a computer issue in the computer lab in the basement of the library. It was obvious that her objective was to find a guy with whom to have children, so she pursued me. I did not show interest. In fact, I did not return most of her phone calls. When her pursuit did not work, she casted a spell on me using Black Magic. I learned about this through two low-life psychics. A few months later, Terry-Anne admitted to having done the deed.

The third person did me in was Eméfa. I met her in Ewomé, my mother's native village in Togo in 2000 when I went to visit in the late spring season. We spoke for only two or three minutes, but she decided that I was the one for her. Like Hawa, her mother and grandmother encouraged her to use negative souls from other dimensions to make me hers. This girl and her family went as far as to perform an actual marriage ceremony for us without my knowledge. I even learned later that she created a figure of me made out of clay. If that is not obsession, then I don't know what is.

The next person who was definitely part of the gang of culprits was my grandmother. This woman was so wicked that every once in a while she killed off one of her children "to eat" as meat with her witchcraft friends. This was not a literal eating of human meat. They would first trap the person's soul into an animal, say a goat or a chicken. Then, they would kill the animal and eat it. When the animal dies, the person also dies soon after. My grandmother was directly involved in my brother Essevi's death. This you will understand later Reader. Furthermore, she was indirectly involved in my father's death. My father's younger sister, Liza, did not even have a chance. She died in my grandmother's room at the age of 33.

As I think back to how she met my grandfather, I am convinced that she used Black Magic to win him over. He met her in the woods, the same path he always took to go to his farm. According to my oldest aunt, my grandfather was not interested at first, but my grandmother was persistent. It is a miracle that my grandfather lived to be ninety-something years old.

Later, after returning to the States, I would understand without a shadow of a doubt that the women were all involved in bringing me down.

I brought my mind back to the Peruvian jungle.

While walking to the main lounge, I saw don Jose. He informed me that there had been an accident, and that his son, don Herberto could not be here today. He said that his fingers were knocked out of place. His head was hit in several places. Apparently, they were on the motorcar in Iquitos when a big dog crossed their vehicle. That was the reason why doña Rcilia had to leave early in the morning unannounced. She was called upon because she knew how to put the fingers back in their places,. Fortunately, the doctors said that Herberto's head injuries were not serious.

July 14, at 1:47 p.m.:

Doña Rcilia, Jose's wife, and I were having Tuesday night's post Ayahuasca discussion. They started the session by asking me to describe the vision that I had. I told them about the darkness—the negative entities' world, and proceeded by describing what I experienced during the last vomit. During the description, I clarify for them what was happening inside my head.

"Do you remember the noise I was making?"

"Yes," doña Rcilia replied.

"Well, that was the entity holding onto my head. I felt it physically in and around my head. It had to become physical…What was interesting about the experience was that it was easy to vomit them. It came so easily that I wasn't really in control. It was as if some other force was at work here. The force definitely did not come from me. I wonder what it was. Maybe it was you, Herberto, or Mother Ayahuasca. I don't know. What do you think it was?"

"It was Mother Ayahuasca," doña Rcilia answered with confidence.

"I still have palpitations in my buttocks, in my biceps," I said pointing to the locations, "and also in the back of my upper legs and a little in my upper left chest. Are these the last remaining entities?" I asked.

"No, they are all gone."

"Then what are the palpitations?"

I did not receive an answer. I left it alone, though I was not convinced she was right.

Friday, July 15, 2011:

It was Friday morning. Today is my brother Essevi's birthday. He would have been thirty-three years old today.

Happy birthday Essevi!

Overall, my day was relaxing. I did not do much. I wrote, took a nap and cried. It was great. I was walking in the woods, heading back to my casita when I felt the tears. Soon after, it occurred to me again that my journey here is almost over. I wanted to believe that what remains is merely my body forgetting that it had been hurt as doña Rcilia said. She also said that the palpitations were never the negative entities "traveling" through my body. According to her, "It was my body telling me that it was suffering." Though I knew that not everything she said was accurate, I found her explanation most intriguing, for how often do we ignore our bodies and how we feel? Too often! And that's part of the reason why we are suffering.

This was the second night I spent alone. It has been a bit lonely. The nights seemed long. My brother Essevi has been around, especially in my head area. So, in essence, I have not really been alone. Mother Ayahuasca also kept me company with her melodious chants.

After our usual spiritual ritual purification session in the evening, doña Rcilia and I headed back to the main compound.

"I'm going to force a vomit tonight even if none voluntarily comes."

"Bueno," she answered.

"It's to make sure there isn't anything else hiding in my body."

It was about 8 p.m. when I returned to my room. Rcilia came back about an hour and a half later for the Ayahuasca session. I was looking forward to putting an end to all of this, because Ayahuasca, as I explained, tastes really nasty. I did not feel this the first time I took it, but I definitely did the subsequent times.

About an hour into the ceremony, I summoned up my strength—from my stomach to both of my temples to vomit. I did it several times. Normally, I would feel the demons resisting physically in my head. However, this time I felt nothing. I did not have any visions or dreams that evening.

The light mattress was falling on me. I pushed it on the wall behind me. This session was utterly different in that a part of my unconscious was trying to figure out a deeper message.

I went outside. For about a minute I was aware of an extraordinary intuition. I could feel the ground being alive—possessing an inner intelligence—a soul, despite its silence. My mind was baffled. Instead of shutting up, it interjected—trying to understand how the ground *feels*. Eventually, the awesomeness of the moment rendered my mind silent.

The ground smiled at me! I was dumbfounded in that brief moment, but I was utterly aware to the core of my essence that it could feel like I can, for I *saw* and *felt* that It too could perceive intuitively as I could mentally. Was this my intent to understand how vegetables *feel* being answered through this entity—the ground? The ground actually smiled at me! My eyes widened in stupefaction. It was undoubtable—my mind had absolutely no questions. This would be what don Juan in Carlos Castaneda's books would call "silent knowledge." It was like the time my soul exited the body and watched the physical vehicle from my desk area with the dark inter-dimensional entity by my left at the foot of the bed.

"How do you *feel*?" I asked meekly.

My question was not answered. My heart quickened for the desire for more silent knowledge, but none came. This was one of the most massive experiences I would ever have on this planet, so I thought.

Much later in November in 2011 in my kitchen, I would stare out the small window, looking at the plant outside and think: "If you can perceive like me, then you have the potential to feel like me."

As I stood outside, I felt at that moment that the dizzy effect of the tobacco was much stronger than the dizzy effect of the Ayahuasca. Once the smoke had gone from my lower throat, I began thinking again about how the demons had blocked my visions. I started with the vision that I had in 2007 that conveyed to me that I was going to die in a plane explosion. As I lied down in my bed in the Amazon jungle, it came to me. After the plane exploded, I briefly saw my own bright white light. The demons did not want me to remember this because if I had recollected, that would have brought them down much sooner, for I would have understood quicker that there is no death.

During the second to the last Ayahuasca session, something wonderful happened that confirmed for me that I was closing this chapter in my life. It began when I was lying flat on my back. I heard music to the north of my head. My logical mind kicked in.

Where in the world is this music coming from?

It was a drum with a tune. It was not too loud or too soft. I quickly shifted my head to Rcilia's direction. The music was not there. A minute or so when my mind had forgotten about it, it came back. It was amazing.

It can't be coming from inside my head or ears or can it?

I moved my ears about. A mosquito was annoying me. I swatted at my right ear. The music definitely was not coming from my mind. I had a hard time believing that Rcilia couldn't hear it. Then suddenly, I had a déjà-vous. I had already seen or been here before. The music! It was not new!

Clarity seized my mind. The demons! They were blocking this part of my vision.

Agbessi, render yourself to the music! You'll have plenty of time to analyze this later.

I focused on the beat of the drum, letting it consume me. Suddenly, I saw myself in Kpalimé on a wide road and the music was still playing. Then, I heard Rcilia singing. I went out to the door's threshold, hoping to feel the calm that I felt two days ago. No, nothing! It was the mapacho.

"The mapacho increases the effect of the Ayahuasca," I recalled Bryant saying during one of the ceremonies."

The hypnotic state! Magnífico! I shouted in my mind. I opened my eyes to look at doña Rcilia. She was singing. I put my left arm up to signal to her that I understood everything and that everything was going to be alright, and that she could stop the ceremony, but she continued.

I looked out of the back screen. I saw what would ordinarily be green plants and weeds. But from my mental state of perception, there was a haze about them. My mind was distorting what the actual plants were, but I was totally conscious of this. The sparkle about them turned into some sort of shadow, and they looked like little plant monsters. Still, there seemed to have been something more to the plants—their inner essence. I wanted to know what they really were minus the illusion. I was comfortable where I was sitting and did not want to get up. Besides, I was still dizzy.

Get up! No! Later! Agbe, when is it the right time to ever explore truth? Stop putting it off. If you can't do it in this life time, then when can you do it?

I went and observed the plants and then returned to my mat. *Be decisive!* The focus is on you, not other people or beings who bring their negativity. The key is not to focus so much on changing others, but yourself *now! Now Agbessi!*

My mind shifted, for doña Rcilia's chant was becoming very hypnotizing.

Listen! It is calculated. It's a calculated illusion to manipulate, but you are always free to decide.

Herberto's plea came back to me: "Focus Agbe!"

Images of humanity in a trance, sleep state came to me again.

The melody! Concentrate!

Waves of negative energy amassed in my throat again. I brushed them off. Then, I heard myself saying out loud:

"Go back to where you came. This is my world not yours."

Then I became more determined.

You didn't focus for most of your life. You were distracted. Sometimes you focused on the loudest thing—the most obvious, but what about the subtle things? They lurk in the shadows. Sometimes you can't see them, but if you concentrate you will catch on.

My mind started judging itself.

Look at you, you didn't even know that you had demons inside of you.

Doña Rcilia blew out a breath as if to tell me to do the same. I read this as a hypnotic suggestion. The other melodies, where are they coming from? The roof, toward the front of the other casita! Amazing! Everything is a calculated suggestion! Suggestions to keep us in a limited state of awareness, to keep us as slaves!

Then came a big wave of intuitive awareness: *The calculated suggestions are an illusion to keep us from reaching the Most Pure, the purest part of ourselves. These are pity pleasures!*

Soon after, I was reliving visions again. I was observing a discarnate entity, which I had seen before in a vision before coming to the jungle but did not quite remember. The impact of these visions would be so strong that months later, I would still be in utter awe and pose the question: "Can I too one day do this?"

As soon as I started forming thoughts, I was stopped. Questions about politics, religions, culture, multinational corporations, money, luxury, and so forth were not even completed before my mind, was shut down again.

"It's all a distraction."

The voice, whose source I was not sure of, was definitely as pure as I have ever felt from any being. Perhaps it belonged to Mother Ayahuasca. The voice was not even needed because I felt the positive vibration directly. This was much akin to the time I was able to read and sense the energy of the dark inter-dimensional entity that materialized in my bed in 2009.

Topic after topic finally rendered me to silence and my mind became quiet as I observed a few discarnate beings (i.e., none physical, fluid form) flying just above the surface of the Earth). The immensity of the fear was stunning. I turned my attention to one particular discarnate entity in the center of my view. It looked like some sort of flying animal, not exactly a snake. It was so, so afraid. The word *fear* does not even begin to describe his emotional or spiritual state. I felt the enormity with which this being vibrated without words. I felt a little sorry for him. He was like a child about to wet his pants. I was utterly aware that this being was at the top of the shadow people who are controlling planet Earth. From this vantage point, I was able to understand that the centers of Light (i.e., powers) on this planet were also here helping these fallen beings.

"This was what I was afraid of?...These were the kinds of beings who terrorized me?" I thought to myself.

This experience compelled me to accept the fact that the rabbit hole does indeed go deep. Divide and conquer is an overall system of distraction that knows no boundaries. It manifests through languages, religions, cultures, gender bias, and the current economic system that we have in the world. In terms of this system, we lie to each other by giving different names to it. We call it capitalism, socialism, and so forth. We are allowing our governments of the world to wreak violence and world wars, and negating that we are enslaving ourselves. What is at stake is your ultimate freedom. If you yourself continue to vote for and or support and maintain a system of dark, raw energy which I call evil, then you are violating, raping Mother Earth. What you will eventually have is hell upon the Earth, a world as I experienced it during the Ayahuasca state. This, I put my soul on. The dark entities have destroyed their world and are now doing the same thing with this planet.

I went back inside the room, to Rcilia's beautiful Shipibo singing. "*This would be the last time I will hear it in a long time to come or never,*" I thought to myself. I sat up. Try as I might, I could not vomit any more demons.

Surely, you remember when you exited your body that auspicious day.

Suddenly, I could not breathe. Rcilia's smoke was too much.

"Air! May I step out to breathe?"

"Yes," she answered.

I stood on the ledge looking at the horizon. The moonlight is very bright. I put my head down, still holding onto the edge of the door. A small feeling of nausea came over me. I waited for a moment, but it never came to fruition. I raised my head again, staring into the void and the green plants. It was dead silent.

Why did you feel lonely the previous day sleeping alone in the woods. The plants? They are a part of you.

I had the feeling that everything was linked to each other, and that I was a part of that oneness. I was perfectly content just standing there and enjoying the plants and the insects' chirping. I had the distinct desire to spread my body on the ground and make myself one with everything.

So calm and peaceful! This is how it is supposed to be—the world.

When the experience was over, I looked toward the entrance of my mother's old casita. There seemed to be some sort of a skeleton figure at the door's threshold.

A skeleton woman? No, there is nothing there. I must be hallucinating!

I looked away for a few seconds, and then turned back. I stared at it for a while. The figure became a little more defined.

A woman? Get out of here. It cannot be a woman. No way!

I went back to the casita. A minute or two later, doña Rcilia ended the Ayahuasca ceremony. I took my flashlight.

"Tell me I'm not going crazy," I told her in Spanish.

I lit my flashlight across the field. A light flashed back. There was indeed a person there, but it was a guy.

"We always have guardians stationed outside for protection," doña Rcilia said.

"I knew I was not going crazy!" I told her.

When I got into the shower to take my cold bath that night, I heard two distinct music of the night: the beating of the drum and Mother Ayahuasca's chant. She sang very close to my ears on and off. And when this was not happening, the triumphant music played to my east. Eventually, I fell asleep. I woke up several times, but the last time I was given another type of music—the rain.

The journey is now nearly over. This was definitely not what I was expecting when I came on this trip. I expected to receive life's greatest mysteries about the nature of existence. Instead, I learned about how *evil* really feels. For most of my life, I thought evil was a religious word. Fortunately, I also learned that love is the greatest source of power and it is always enough. I do have two lingering thoughts. The first is: If I had allowed myself to sink deeper and deeper into the entities' world of darkness, would I have discovered the origin of evil? That was certainly not something I was ready to explore. The darkness was too overwhelming.

My second thought concerns the answers that I did not get. I did not receive any answers about reincarnation nor did I learn anything about the illusion of the split of Infinity.

That same morning as I sat in the rocking chair in my room, I heard myself say out loud:

"I have to quit my job. It is not spiritually fulfilling."

I have thought about it a lot in 2010-11, but now the feeling is much stronger. I wanted to do something that actually changes the consciousness of the planet for the better. I could no longer continue helping to advance a spiritually dead system: the formal education system. In the grand scheme of things, I knew I was making very little difference in my fellow soul mates' lives. That morning, I gave myself a few years before quitting my job.

Saturday, July 16, 2011

Today, I made every effort to learn as much about Black Magic as I could. I asked don Jose to tell me about the Shipibo Indians and shamanism in Peru. He promised that he would but could not do it right then because he was busy with his work and that we had a long day ahead of us. We indeed had a lot to do that day. I had to go to Iquitos and see about my hotel reservation, for which I had not paid. The day's journey began with our ride in the motorcar to his house in Iquitos. The ride took about two hours.

I made every effort to talk to his wife apropos what she knew about Black Magic. I was lucky, for she told me about her first experience when she was a child. She sat opposite to me in the vehicle.

"My father was traditional. I wanted to go to school, but he wanted me to get married and to have children. In those days, husbands took care of their wives…I really wanted to learn to speak Spanish. My aunt, who was a teacher said she would teach me. One day, we went to…There was an old man there. He said, 'I am widowed and alone, you could be my wife.'"

I smiled.

"He wanted to marry you? How old were you?"

"I was eight years old."

"And he wanted to *marry* you?" I asked in surprise, "How crazy."

"He didn't care. He said I was pretty, and he needed a wife. He had an illness, a big lump on his shoulders. I told him that he was an old sick man and that I didn't want him. I became sick after I left. There was something in my throat. I coughed out nasty stuff. My father took me to the hospital. The doctors didn't see anything wrong with me, but I was sick."

"He cursed you."

"He was a witch. My father did not want to take me to a traditional medicine man because he was evangelical."

"An evangelical Christian?"

"Yes," she answered as we passed a very nice house on our left.

"That's a very nice house someone has there," I commented.

"It's not a house. It's a missionary."

"Catholic?"

"No, evangelical... When I slept that evening, I heard a voice. I told my parents about it. The next day when I was asleep, I heard the voice again. It was the old man's. I recognized it. He came to visit me…My parents said that I was lost to them: I was going to die. My father went to confront the *brujo*. He was not afraid of him. He told him that if I died, he would also die."

"Do you mind if I put this in the book? This is all very fascinating."

"Yes, you can."

"I heard a similar story in Mexico. How did you heal?"

"My aunt took me to a healer. He took out a fish bone in my throat."

"Did the old man touch you when you saw him the first time?"

"No."

"So he learned enough to cast the curse without touching you. Interesting."

We arrived at their house about forty or fort-five minutes later. Jose told me that I would be accompanied by two women to do my errands in the city. They were two of his daughters: Esther and Eunice, whom I had met the first day. We took a motorcar taxi. We had difficulty finding Hobo Travelers Hotel at first. I had to use the internet to look up the address again. When we finally found it, everything went alright with the payment.

We ate lunch and returned to don Jose's house. There, I was invited to the main room where everybody gathered. I was introduced to the rest of Jose's beautiful daughters, and then we left a few minutes later. I observed the town and compared it to living conditions in Togo. There was much resemblance—perhaps a little less green here. Don Jose made a stop and went to a house to the left of the road. He came back to report that Herberto was still not feeling well enough to attend the night's ceremony. I told him that it was alright, and that I wanted to go say hello to him before we left.

"This is my wife, Mercy," Herberto said.

Nice choice, I thought to myself.

Herberto began telling me about his "accident," and it soon became evident to me that the family did not tell me the whole story as not to worry me.

"How are you feeling Agbe?"

"How are *you* feeling?" I answered with a question.

"My arms, head, and legs were swollen. I'm fine now…Recall that I told you that the black man in the vision told me to watch out if I helped you?"

"He was the cause of this? What happened exactly?"

"I dropped Bryant off at the airport and was going back to my house to get something…There was a big dog, rather big. It cut in front of me and turned left. I was moving, not knowing it was going to come back. I pressed the break and held onto it as well as I could, but I was thrown off the bike. I flipped over and became unconscious.

"I was surrounded by the rock," he said.

He had fainted. When he woke up, he was surrounded by faces looking at him. The dog was dead.

"There weren't any fractures in my body, but my head was swollen this big," he said, illustrating with his hand. He also illustrated how swollen his legs and arms were.

"His powers came from books."

"How do you know that?" I asked.

"When you come across beings, they ask you who you are, and you in turn ask them who they are. When this happens, you're able to see other things. I saw three piles of books, dark books. That's where he got his powers from. Some get it from rocks."

All this was very fascinating to me.

How does one get powers from a simple stone or a rock?

I remembered the scientific periodic table. Every element is not only in human beings, but some could also be found in inanimate objects such as rocks.

"Then what happened?" I asked impatiently, "The black man appeared with his two headed snake?"

"No, remember that I had taken out the eyes of the one with the monstrous-looking face?"

"Yes, so only the other appeared then?"

"He said, 'I warned you not to help him.' I told him that I was fine, that it was just my body that was hurt. He came toward me a little and I pointed at his forehead, and half of his face turned into blood. It peeled off and all you could see were bones on one side."

I felt Herberto was holding back on me. One does not just point and injure another without a weapon.

"I don't quite understand. You said you pointed at him and that happened?"

Before he could answer, I posed another question.

"Did you use a weapon from your soul? Your Light Self?"

He saw that I knew more than the average person, so he went into details.

"A light went out of my finger and into his forehead. He said he was sorry and then he left."

"He left?"

"He said he lost and the battle was over."

So you used a light energy source from your body to defeat him," I said, "Most people don't know they have weapons inside their souls.

"How do you feel?" he asked me again.

"I am impressed that the impossible has been accomplished. A miracle has happened. I am also, uhm—" I said, searching for the word "proud" in Spanish, "I am very happy that you chose to be brave. As I told doña Rcilia yesterday, what you guys are doing is as important as and sometimes even more important than the work of medical doctors. Remember that. Remember that there will be a lot more challenges to come with every lighter consciousness. That is, as we advance higher, dimension after dimension, we will encounter other challenges. You must remember that no matter how much we suffer, we must stay the course because if it takes a thousand years, the rewards are fantastic. I had a glimpse of the beauty of this when I came out of my body in 2009. I was not asleep when it happened…I am happy to have found good souls to help me."

"Gracias," he said sincerely.

"No, gracias a usted. There is something that I have not told you. That first night when we did the ceremony, my soul rose above my head during the session, and as it stood there watching Rcilia, trying to understand her, I saw Mother Ayahuasca to my left in a form of a huge anaconda. Normally, I would have selected a weapon from my soul to defend myself, but I felt no such need. I felt that she was safe. There was no need for words."

His eyebrows rose as if he were surprised I knew that.

"You can feel intentions and vibes at the spiritual level and that suffices…"

"I will make every effort to be at your last Ayahuasca session."

"It's alright if you can't make it."

The cell phone rang, and it was his brother. He told his wife to hand it to his father so that our conversation could continue.

"Don't forget to write the report for Francesco about your experience."

"No problem. I was thinking about putting it in my book. Do you mind?"

No, it's a good idea," he answered, pleased.

"There's one thing to be mindful of. Once people hear about this place, a lot more will come. My advice is to be careful of who you share your shamanic secrets with: especially the shamanic apprentices. The thing is, the world is very cruel. Certain Europeans and Americans have come into our countries before and have learned everything from the old and the shamans and then destroyed them. When I say 'our countries,' I mean developing countries. These shamans have gone underground to keep their knowledge hidden. So, as you heal people, beware of those who may have bad intentions."

"Thank you for your advice. Mercy, please give him some water."

His wife handed me a bottle, which read "sin gas."

"Do you have one with 'con gas'?" I asked.

She brought me one with bubbles and I left to go wait in the car for his father to return.

Sunday, July 17, 2011:

I woke up with the same happy question and answer:

Is it enough? It's always enough.

I understood completely how I was able to devise the so-called neutrality strategy. It was so simple. Love! I was influenced by the love that my brother and father showed me. No one had ever loved me that deeply before. They came everyday to check up on me in the middle of the night, to defend me when the inter-dimensional entities were pursing me. And even after two years when the entities were gone, my brother still hung around everyday to make sure I was alright. To say that I was inspired by love would be an understatement. I was empowered by love, and was trying to understand it; for, never in my life had anyone shown me so much commitment. This feeling as well as my spiritual experiences compelled me to reconsider what my own Light is worth…

Tuesday, July 19, 2011:

I did not report on yesterday because nothing really important happened. Well, my jaguar friend did come into my room around five o'clock in the morning from the roof. Apparently, he had been trying all night. I heard noises, but I ignored them thinking that they were caused by other night creatures.

I am leaving today after lunch, but I still have not heard don Jose's story yet.

At about 11 a.m. we heard the motorcar. Ninfa, Herberto's ex-wife said that don Jose was home. The dog started barking. I stopped my conversation to go see who had arrived. To my pleasant surprise, Herberto was walking my direction with the aid of a crouch (i.e., a walking stick). His right foot was plastered. I ran a couple of errands and then returned to the living room. By then a meeting was called to say our final farewell. A minute or two later, Herberto came to join us. Though everybody was there sitting with us, Herberto and I dominated the conversation as we caught up on all the things we did not discuss as a result of the accident. I had a lingering question that I posed him about the black magician, and from there we went into details. The dialogue started with me asking:

"What exactly is the being who attacked you? Was he really summoned from another dimension?"

"Yes and no. He is part of the man who sent him."

"How is he a part of the man who sent him?"

"He is part of his energy system."

"He is him, but not? I am not understanding. Are you saying that the person who sent him is controlling him from afar? From West Africa?"

"Not exactly. The Moreno is not the original. He is a part of him. It's a little difficult to explain."

He pointed to his mother and father.

"My parents are mostly 'ordinary.' They are not shamans. When a shaman does a plant diet, he acquires protection and powers. The energy of the plant becomes part of his power system."

"His energy system?"

"Yes, with the diet, the shaman acquires protection from the plant. When the black man came that evening, he asked who I was."

"How did you know it was alright to face him in combat?"

"It's really simple. Before engaging in a battle, a shaman first finds out if he can take on the being before him. I inquired about the black man and I was able to see how powerful he was. He showed me his powers, which came from books. Powers that come from books are not as powerful as powers that come from plants. So, that was when I decided I could defeat him. If I could not have succeeded, then I would have told you that I was not strong enough to heal you, and I would have told you to go to a more powerful shaman who could defeat him.

"Let me give you an example. My uncle was a top shaman. One day, he was celebrating with his family…he had a beer and went home. Later, a neighbor sought his help to aid his father. My uncle told him that he could not help, and to go see another shaman, and that he had been drinking. He explained to him that he was not in a good state of mind to help, but the son insisted, saying that he was the best and that the hospital doctors could not do anything. He persuaded my uncle and he went with him. There, he saw the old man lying down, sick. He drank some Ayahuasca —"

"His own?" I interrupted, thinking that there might be some trickery involved here.

"His own. He saw a vision of the shaman-sorcerer who had casted the spell. The sorcerer showed him his powers and my uncle understood that the brujo was about at the same level he was, so he proceeded. He healed the man. However, he did not take into account that the beer he had drunken lowered his powers. The next morning, he was still in a dizzy, trance state. At 3 p.m. he was still dazed. A few days passed and he was still in that world. His children could not get him out of that world. They went to a very good shaman who could not do it. Six months later, he died. So you see, it's simple. A shaman knows when he can heal or not heal."

"Bueno, now, what about the African guy who sent the being? Will he know what happened?"

"He may become sick, but may not know that Agbe has been healed. He might get a vision of me, but he will only see my face. He won't see my body because I'm protected by the rock. There's nothing he can do."

"Alright, there's something that I have never understood. Why would you cast a spell on someone and have the person be possessed by demons? What purpose does that serve?

The demons were inside causing me pain, but how does that help them get what they want? I have not been able to understand it."

"I don't understand it either," Herberto said, leaning back a little in his seat.

"Alright, I know that the demons were sent by Hawa, her mother and her oldest aunt. Actually, it started in 2001 and this girl also said that I would only marry her. Now, Hawa and her mother and aunt also said the same thing. But, how does my suffering help them marry their daughter? Because I said no. I had the will power to do it.

Herberto leaned forward as if thinking.

"Now that you mentioned it, I did have a brief vision of seven well dressed, well-mannered girls who were approaching you, but could not get through."

He paused briefly, and then continued.

"Seven doesn't literally mean seven…It can mean a lot more. The black man with the snake was sent to prevent you from finding healing, and frightening women out of your life."

As his hand ascended to illustrate this, a flash of intuition dawned on me.

"Because he was in me, he was able to do it whenever I came into contact with the women. Ha, ha! Brilliant! It makes sense! He frightened her away—the last one. She said she was having these strange dreams. She was the most unfortunate because I thought it would really work. I thought the love would be enough."

I gave myself a moment of silence to brood.

Love is always enough, but when fear gets in the way, one does not see clearly. She gave into fear, not love.

My mind switched to all the women who have casted dark magic spells on me to be with them. They went to a specialist, and they paid him or her. It is their job. They derive income from this job; so they do it, negating the signs that every ill-will must eventually be answered for, no exceptions. The women who asked for the spell to be casted do not understand the mechanism of the dark arts. Every single one of these women I have come across went to church, and was either a catholic or a Christian. They went to church to "worship" God, but yet behind closed doors they were doing something else. What once astonished me is that these same "God-loving people" chastised me for not going to church. How interesting, the total hypocrisy in their acts.

Several other images flashed into my mind. In all of them, I was at Lehman College at either the computer lab or at the basement of the library. I recalled writing a letter to Hawa when I began to sense a presence. It was clear to me that my correspondence was being read. Now, I am thinking that it might have been this dark being in me. Another possibility sketched upon my mind, but I let it go.

When it was nearing 12 p.m., I reminded don Jose that he did not tell me about "el banco." He promptly took a seat and I joined him.

"My grandparents' told me this," he began.

He asked me if I remembered what a *banco* is and I answered him with "a super shaman, the best of the best." He nodded in agreement. His great grandfather was a Meraya (i.e., a banco).

"Each banco had four helpers. Each helper was also a shaman. El banco was well-known in the community. People went to him for their children and their own health. He took Ayahuasca every evening. He had a big house—5 meters by 10 meters long. At three o'clock in the afternoon, his wife performed a cleansing ritual around the house using

Ayahuasca plants. Then she enclosed the ceremonial place with a mosquetero. During the ceremonies, el banco's soul leaves his body and spirits enter and speak—"

"I'm not understanding."

Herberto was passing by the big casita. The conversation was about to take a detour and focus on one of the essential questions that I had before coming to Peru.

"What are these spirits exactly?"

"Spirits of the plants," don Jose answered.

"You're saying that certain plants have souls just like us?"

"All of them."

As soon as I had posed the question, Mother Ayahuasca came to mind. She works through plants, but has a powerful soul. *So, of course some plants have actual souls.* It was his latter statement that hooked me. I knew that everything is energy and that this world is not really physical, but this was a bit much even for me. Esther, his daughter came to explain.

"The plant spirit can transform into all types of beings," she said. This was far out, and I had difficulty believing it.

"You mean the broccoli that I ate yesterday has a soul?" I asked, looking at don Jose, who did not answer. I had the impression that he was not quite sure about the nuances of his answer.

"Medicinal plants," Esther said.

"All medicinal plants have souls," don Jose reiterated.

"What about that plant outside, behind you?"

"Everything has life," he replied. I already knew that. What I wanted to know was *how* "ordinary" plants and vegetables *feel*. I knew that plants and vegetables do not feel like animals and human beings, but here he was insinuating that medical plants have a soul and may therefore *feel* like us. This was mind boggling for me. Here I was thinking that I was on the right path by not eating meat and fish, and here he was implying that it was impossible not to cause harm to any living creature. This did not quite make sense to me. He continued.

"I was once sick…the plantain liquid, its spirit appeared to me in a dream as my aunt and told me that if I continue with the medicine for two days, I would be healed. It healed me," he said holding the right side of his stomach. Honestly, I didn't catch everything he had just said, for my mind was still on his earlier statement about plants having souls.

"We've diverged from the topic," he said.

"Yes, but this is what I am interested in. It's one of the major questions that I had before coming here. Perhaps to you this may seem silly, but I really want to know how vegetables *feel*."

Don Jose's wife was laughing. Jose continued the story of his ancestor.

"After the ceremony, everybody left. El banco stayed inside the mosquetero, singing without eating for a month. Then Ayahuasca leaves started growing in his hands. Two months later, his wife noticed that he was becoming a plant—. Three months later, he became an Ayahuasca plant."

"What happened to his family?"

"His wife and children moved away. Later, a shaman came to cut him. The banco was no more. Don Jose went on to explain to me how the banco's spirit shared many secret knowledge with the shaman who cut him down.

"There aren't any more bancos left today."

"They took their knowledge with them to the grave," Esther added.

"Esther and Eunice know a lot about the story. Let them tell you the rest so that I can go back to the job."

"Tell me about the Shipibos," I requested, looking at Esther and her sister.

"They were very shy. They communicated through their drawings," she said, pointing to a garment her mother was wearing. I looked at the drawings on it. They had similar designs to my wrist band—the Ayahuasca symbols.

"Where are the Shipibos from?"

"They are originally from Pucallpa, not Iquitos. Los Boras, Los Quito, Yahuas, and Hitotos are originally from Iquitos. But now there are a lot of Shipibos here."

"What percentage of Peruvians is Shipibo?"

She did not know. I told her not to worry about it, and that I could easily find out using the internet.

"In my mother's time, there were Shipibo teachers. They are the only ones to preserve their culture."

"Do you learn to write and speak Shipibo in school?"

"Only in primary school. Most of us speak it. That's what's important. We wear our clothes."

"So, I am Shipibo now. I have the clothes your parents made for me."

She smiled. The conversation was interrupted by her mother who was complaining that lunch time had passed and the cook did not serve me my meal yet. It was 1:37 p.m., thirty-seven minutes past my lunch time. A few minutes later, I ate and went back to my casita to prepare for my departure.

On the way to Iquitos, I considered Herberto's explanations about the being that had caused his accident. I arrived at one conclusion: The mere fact that I changed my diet has given me a certain amount of energy protection regardless of the plant diet. This was fascinating. I interpreted all this as: food gives energy and energy is a form of protection regardless of the plant diet. So, I was right. What you eat can provide you spiritual protection from negative entities. By the same token, if you eat low level energy food such as meat, fish and drink hard liquor, then that opens up your aura for negative entities to enter your body and possess you. No spells or Black Magic needed.

CHAPTER 8

RETURN TO EL MUNDO MÁGICO

After what transpired in the Amazon rainforest of Peru, two very important concepts, *freedom and love*, began to occupy my mind.

In terms of freedom, the very idea that humanity is free now seems utterly ludicrous to me. How can one be free when one is enslaved? When one lives in a system that blinds one from knowing one's ultimate Light Self? One cannot. Freedom comes from the greater awareness that we human beings are really Light beings—Gods, just like animals and plants. It is the global understanding that we are not our physical bodies. It is an undying universal fact that we are genderless. It is the recognition that our formal education, economic, political, military, religious, and health care systems are not only fundamentally flawed, but were set up to enslave us. It is no accident that human beings think they are biological beings or merely sons and daughters of God.

In addition to freedom, my conception of the very meaning of love has expanded, and later I would ask *What is love?* This question has been posed over the ages. Does it have an age limit? Can love be felt between children? From an adult to a child? Can animals give love? What do we grab onto that can endure longer than physical sex, anger, resentment, and hate? Is love merely a feeling? Electrical signals going to the brain? *NO!* We can recognize it even if we cannot identify it. Love knows form and no form that is intelligent, that does not seek to control. Its subtleties last forever, though the conscious mind may not be fully aware of it at first. Love protects and casts away demons. The flicker of pure light is love. It is the ultimate solution to escaping from the third and *all* slave dimensions. When I first wrote the first draft of this book, I did not include this section about love nor the little girl that I will talk about soon. These experiences remind me that love comes in all disguises and that I was "grabbing" onto it unconsciously without being consciously aware of it. Thus it was for me as I entered the hotel.

Sandra was holding a little girl who appeared to be her daughter. Sandra's mother was entering the living room. Before I explain what happens next, let me say that two weeks had passed since I had shaven my beard. By then it had fully grown and was ugly looking, especially near the neck area. It was with this "monstrous" look that I approached Sandra and her daughter.

"Hola," I said.

Sandra smiled, trying to get her daughter to do the same. She maintained a cautious look. I went nearer, trying to salute her with a handshake. She stared right into my face, and I moved a little closer. To my surprise, she started crying.

"It's the beard," I told Sandra.

I ascended up the concrete stairs.

A few hours after working on this second book in my hotel room, I shaved and went downstairs. I said hello to the little girl again. She gave me a smile as an answer.

The time was about 11:30 a.m. I was in the hotel in Iquitos. I opened up a bottle of organic wine—35 South—that I brought with me from New York. I poured myself a glass and the strangest thing happened—my taste has noticeably altered. This is absolutely one of the most bizarre things that has happened to me in a long time. The wine not only tasted differently, but my desire to consume it has also diminished slightly. Was I placating the demons before? Was I drinking for them? How about what I ate? Has my taste for ordinary food also changed? My diet has basically been the same since my Ayahuasca program. I have not consumed much salt, oil, sugar or pepper.

A day or two after arriving in Iquitos I went out in the evening in search of a Brazilian artist recommended by Sandra. By luck, I found him at La Plaza de Armas. I told him that I wanted a painting and or a drawing of a vision that I had. A lot of people gathered around him to watch as he worked. A young man in his twenties sat to my right and asked me where I was from. I told him Lima, Peru. He did not know whether or not to believe me, probably because he could not place my Spanish accent. I smiled and told my artist to focus on the Light Being to the right. I did not tell him at that time that the drawing was for my first book. He assumed that my vision came from my Ayahuasca experience. My new friend Steve took interest in the drawing.

"Are you catholic?" he asked.

"No, I'm from the Universe."

I got a smile out of him.

"That's me in the bed, and that's my soul to the right. To the left is a dark entity in fluid form, scratching its head, trying to figure out why it can't enter my physical body."

"Have you ever heard of schizophrenia?" he asked, taking a cheap shot at me. I smiled.

"This really happened."

He seemed evermore confused.

"Have you ever tried Ayahuasca?"

"No."

"You're from Peru and you haven't? You do know that there's a lot more than this physical world, right?"

"Are you religious?" he asked, still trying to ground me in a particular belief system.

"What's your religion?" I asked him in turn.

"Buddhist."

"Well, the Light inside you can choose anything ello wants to experience. It's not above or below anything. This life is a temporary experience. I came here for healing. I have been searching for years and years, and this was the only place I found it. So, you've never tried Ayahuasca. Do you have Native American blood in you?"

"Yes, but I only speak Spanish."

"You've never learned your Indian language?"

He shook his head.

"I'm not big on culture or religion, but some things are worth preserving. I see these cultures disappearing. A guy at the hotel said that young people in this country don't value their Indian culture. With the disappearance of certain cultures and languages, so goes the knowledge. I'm originally from Togo."

"How many languages do you speak?"

"Four. I'm Ewe. When I go to my country, I mostly speak Ewe, my native language."

"Where's Togo?" the artist asked.

"Next to Ghana, West Africa."

"This is the most racist country in Latin America. When you ask for something, they don't take you seriously. But, when a gringo asks, they are pleased and rush to him," the artist said.

"You're saying that this is the most racist country in Latin America?" I asked, trying to confirm.

"Yes, it's not like that in Brazil, Columbia, or Argentina," he answered confidently. I was not sure, for I have heard some very unpleasant things about Argentina. I looked at him carefully. He had long hair and his skin color was more or less their color.

"Listen, it's the same thing in Togo. They treat me differently once they know that I'm also American. That happens when people value themselves less. It's the system. What's happening in Latin America is no different than what's happening in Africa. There's a connection. People put emphasis on the superficial. As a language teacher, I can tell you that there's a definite bias toward Spanish, French, and English. It's not an accident…Now that's exactly what I am talking about! The Light! Increase the radiance of the Light! That's exactly what I experienced."

He smiled.

The painting was completed and I began walking away when Steve started talking to me. We were now conversing about reincarnation, which he believed, probably because he was Buddhist. He asked me for a few Peruvian soles to take the bus back home. I gave it to him, but the conversation did not end there. It turned to the consumption of food. He was a bit puzzled that I did not eat meat or fish. We were in front of my hotel and he wanted to continue. There was a plant in front of us. He pointed to it and said:

"This plant has a soul; I guess you can't eat it," he said with a smile.

"The question is 'How does the plant *feel*?' I know that animals and people feel alike, but I don't know how the plant—"

"I don't eat that much meat," he said cutting me off. Without thinking, I said, "Listen, even this wall is alive."

He seemed incredulous.

"I don't care what you do. I am not judging you. You are free to do whatever you want. There are degrees," I said, then I stopped myself, for I knew I was talking too much again.

"I'll help you any way I can with coming to America. Good night." We shook hands and he left.

I was beginning to consider the idea that there was no way to get around the whole food thing. No matter what you do, you hurt something.

But vegetables don't have a nervous system, and therefore do not feel like us. But, according to what Jose and what my own intuition is telling me, medicinal plants such as Ayahuasca have souls just like you and I. But yet, we chop them down and combine them with chacruna to make the medicine; and these two plants accept this. Perhaps, I am not pursing the question correctly. What if I make a different conclusion based on the facts before me: medicinal plants such as Psychotria Viridis and Banisteriopsis spp *(i.e.,* Ayahuasca*) do not have a nervous system, but yet they have souls. So, they do not feel pain the same way as animals and human beings. What about trees? How do they feel.*

I stopped myself momentarily to refocus my thoughts

The question is in how—in what manner, not if!

Later, however, all doubts would disappear from my mind. Everything not only has life, but has a soul.

July something, 2011:

I did not remember what the exact date or day was, but Eunice, her sister and I had just exited the hotel gate.

A few seconds later, Sandra came out with her mother and daughter. The little girl had a blank stare on her face. She looked at the two young women and then stared at me. I could not believe it.

"She's jealous," her mother said with a smile. Her grandmother smiled. I was going to walk away, but something told me to be my usual playful self. I went and took her into my arms.

"You know you're the only one for me; always," I said in Spanish.

She smiled and laughed a little. Then she gave me two kisses on both cheeks. I wanted to return the kiss on the *cheek*, but she refused to turn.

"Ok," I said in Spanish. I gave her back to her mother and waved bye to her. As I walked away with the two women, I thought to myself: *Is this the same five-year old girl who was afraid of me a few days ago?*

Tuesday evening, July 19, 2011:

I did not think that I would write anymore about my trip here in Peru, but I have found that the topic of conversations in the last couple of days with people I have come across in Iquitos were not only relevant to the health aspect of the story I am telling, but have a worldly feel to it. This particular conversation began with the hotel manager Sandra. In the late evening of July 19, Sandra walked into the building. I was sitting in a wooden table that was shaped somewhat like a heart, well, at least part of it. I was near the entrance of the hotel which was enclosed with a metal gate. From where I sat one could see cars and motorcars going by. Sandra entered and I struck a conversation with her.

"Have you ever tried Ayahuasca?"

"Yes…"

She explained to me how she became terribly sick one day. Someone had put something into her body using Black Magic.

"My whole body felt like there were worms in it," she said frowning and elevating her right arm to illustrate. "I went to the hospital and the doctor said that I should go see a shaman. It had gotten really bad. I went to see one who was a friend. I didn't want to drink the Ayahuasca, but he told me that he could not help me unless I drank it…Some tourists at the hotel here have asked me about Ayahuasca, and I told them how great it works. They think I'm crazy."

"Did they actually call you crazy?"

"They did not have to, even if they're speaking a different language, you can read their laughter—"

"And their body language," I added.

"Yes. It's funny because they're the ones who asked about it. So, I stop explaining when I am asked now. I just tell them to go try it and see."

"It's no use. It's like talking to the blind. It's something I'm working on—not talking too much. In developed countries such as the U.S., such 'drugs' are looked down upon. It's even worse talking about one's spiritual experiences. This is the first time for me, but the silent ridicule is pervasive in the States. Well, at least here people are more open to it."

"They are not!" she said emphatically, "They don't want anything to do with it. They are not interested in the traditional medicine Peru has to offer. It is foreigners who take interest."

"May I put this in my book?"

"Sure."

"Well, my first book is called A Glimpse of Who We Are. It'll go in my second one. The first one is about who we are beyond the physical body as I have experienced it over and over again from 2007-2009. The second is going to be called Escape from the Third Dimension. It's about issues such as this. It covers traditional medicine, economics—basically the slave state of humanity. It's about how humanity is willingly accepting its own slave system. Take for example the food supply. It is corrupted and manipulated and most people suspect that there is something wrong, but they continue with the madness, the insanity of continuing to consume the poison. Even here in Peru, it's the same thing. People think just because it is labeled "natural" that it is really natural. It is not.

"When I went to the supermarket here this evening, I saw nothing but polluted, chemically altered food."

"I have said to people myself that they're getting sick because of the food they eat—because of the fat. It doesn't make sense, yet they continue eating it.'

"Yeah, you should check out the film Food Inc. Monsanto is poisoning us. You'll see how animals are raised. They don't even have sex anymore. They are injected with chemicals and fed genetically altered food such as corn. Cows eating corn, please! These things rarely make it to the mainstream news. It was, however, on the internet. I just recently found out about it."

"What's Monsanto?"

"It's an American global food corporation that has pretty much taken over the world. They have taken over the supply of food in most countries. India is having a tough time with them now. They control about 90% of the food supply."

"How is that possible? If I don't want to, I just don't buy from them."

"To affect the whole sea, you go to the root—the seeds. Seeds are the root of crops and everything we eat. Affect the seeds through genetic pollution or modification, then you've affected the whole food supply. This company compels farmers to grow crap through legislation in countries. Farmers have no choice because Monsanto controls 90 percent of the seed supply. That's how they are corrupting our food supply globally. It's not normal to be sick. It really isn't. May I tell you what I have learned?"

"Yes."

"I've learned that there's a connection to these different forms of trickery. It's a real conspiracy, but the minute you mention it, people think you're crazy. They are conditioned to jump to that conclusion. John F. Kennedy spoke about this conspiracy theory. The word "conspiracy" was the exact word he used. Soon after, he was assassinated.

"There is a connection to traditional medicine such as Ayahuasca. These things aren't drugs. They help you gain access to who you really are—the Light. The same is true for the food we consume. These multinational corporations understand the importance of eating real natural food (i.e., organic). Chemical-free food allows you to be more aware of the nature of things. If Monsanto were to sell chemical-free food, a lot of companies would be out of business—including pharmacies and hospitals. Hospitals keep people sick so that they can keep treating them for illnesses they should not have in the first place."

The conversation ended soon after and I began translating my first book into Spanish.

Wednesday, July 20, 2011:

In the late afternoon, I sat in the seating area of the hotel talking to Kid and Lucio, my new friends who worked at the hotel. Kid was to the left of me. Lucio was sitting several feet away from me, near the computer area. Sandra's mother passed by. I offered her a mapacho, which she turned down. I had just eaten and wanted to take a nap, but sleep was not coming, so I took out one to smoke. It was only one, but given that I do not smoke cigarettes or cigars, it had a huge dizzy effect on me. I went upstairs to the third floor to take a nap. As I lied down, I knew I definitely should not have smoked an entire tobacco. It rendered me weak energetically, and took away Mother Ayahuasca's precious busy time. I heard her humming her usual protective chant again in my hotel room. When I woke up later that evening, I made a firm promise not to waste her time again. I was, nevertheless, impressed by her love, her dedication. This was the third being with whom I was utterly impressed.

Thursday, July 21, 2011:

I really did not think I would be writing again until I went to California, but this book seems to be taking its own course. This morning while writing in bed, I felt three palpitations in my body. I would have liked to believe Rcilia, that the battle was over, but my doubt had grown. It was now self-evident that demons remain in my body. Doña

Rcilia was able to feel and see some of the negative entities, but she was not able to see within my entire light body.

Presently, I sat to the right of the same place I had conversed with Sandra. I continued my translation project for my first book.

About an hour into the translation of it, my new friend Kid showed up. He sat down and immediately engaged in a conversation with me. Before I knew it, he was telling me his life story. He told me how he grew up with an American gringa who worked in the jungle. He said that she raised him for twelve years, but he wanted to be free.

"My mother worked for her for seventeen years and had never seen Iquitos. She didn't even know that there was so much here."

"It sounds like she worked night and day for this lady."

"That was the only thing she ever did…I could have gone to Florida. The gringa wanted to adopt me. But, I didn't want to. I like it here. Most young people now don't care. They just learn Spanish. They don't speak their native language. They are not interested. It's like they are ashamed."

Interesting! I thought. *This guy was indirectly talking about cultural manipulation through language: the centralization of culture and language.*

This pleased me very deeply, for I was glad he was aware of this. Day after day, I have come across Native Americans who speak their native language in Peru, but the street signs and billboards did not reflect this. Everything was in Spanish. Even the people portrayed on these billboards have no resemblance to the natives.

"So you speak your own language?"

"Yes."

"As a teacher of languages, I can tell you that we promote Spanish as if it were your first language, completely negating your native languages as if they never existed. I've often asked myself where the Native Americans are. Did these languages just disappear? In West Africa where I am originally from, French is quite common. It's manipulating the entire system, now with the spread of television…I grew up speaking Ewe, my native language as all Africans do theirs. I barely spoke three sentences in English before going to the States. When you go to Togo and Ghana now you'll see a significant negative change in the people's perception of themselves. Through television and the radio, the West is heavily importing its cultural garbage. Who would have ever thought that I would see bagging pants in my own remote village in West Africa."

I stopped, for I realized I had become passionate about the topic and was talking too much. I did not want to monopolize the conversation. I waited for him to say something, but it seemed he was absorbing what I was saying.

"So you said that you didn't want to be a slave with this gringa. What did you mean?"

"I like to be free," he said with a smile, leaning back in his chair. I have a lot of time to myself here."

"So, you did not feel that you would be free in Florida?"

"No, I like it here. I grew up in the jungle."

"Have you ever done Ayahuasca in the jungle?"

"I've done Ayahuasca all my life," he said, looking at his legs, "I do other plant diets too. I do…for hunting. Once, someone put a curse on me when I was young, my family went from shaman to shaman. None of them helped me. My left leg was swollen."

"They did not know what was wrong with you?"

"They knew!" he said with a mixture of assurance and a hint of irritation.

"The shamans: the same ones who use Ayahuasca to heal?" I asked trying to ascertain and make the link to Mother Ayahuasca.

"There are a lot of bad shamans. They are after money."

"That makes sense. So what became of your leg?"

"My family found a good shaman to heal me. This time, my mother said she would only pay after she saw me healed."

"Let's go back to what you were saying earlier about shamans using Ayahuasca to do bad things."

"Mother Ayahuasca has many 'ingenious.'"

"What do you mean?"

"Soldiers."

"And you mean they are bad?"

"They use their knowledge to cast curses."

This was where the conversation became really exciting and before I knew it, I found myself defending Mother Ayahuasca.

"Mother Ayahuasca would not allow such evil under her name. I have seen her, in one of her forms. She has a good soul," I said emphatically and passionately. Steve, who was to my left nodded with a smile.

The conversation with Kid would resume later in the evening, but for now I left him to attend to my dinner. After dinner, I found Steve sitting on the second floor by the staircase. He also spoke to me about Black Magic and rocks. I offered him a mapacho and went to eat my granola cereal. I returned after eating to converse with him some more. He smoked and told me about the rock on the second floor staircase area where he was working. According to him, the rock walked to the bathroom and downstairs on the first floor. He said he put the rock back in its location several times, but he kept finding it by the bathroom and the first floor. He was laughing. He was convinced the spirit of the rock had displaced itself without anyone moving it.

"So, who exactly is Mother Ayahuasca? Is she just in charge of the plants here in Peru?"

"She's in charge of plants in the jungle all over like Brazil."

Late that afternoon, I found myself engrossed in another fantastic conversation about medicinal plants. At the time, I had no idea that it was nicely set up by the positive powers that be. I do not recall how our conversation commenced, but I do remember congratulating my new friend about not going to graduate school. He had considered doing his master's, but could not come to terms with the astronomical costs and the fact that he suspected that it was "just a piece of paper."

"Money is just numbers on a computer screen…," I said.

"I like you," he said laughing.

Somehow or another the conversation turned to medicinal plants.

"Have you ever tried other hallucinogenic substances?" he asked me.

"No, this is my first one. Well, I had some marijuana cookies."

It was obvious to me that he had taken other "drugs."

"You've tried Peyote?"

He smiled.

"Mescalito has a very strong masculine energy. You'll never forget."

"Does it give you spiritual protection?"

"Yes," he answered with confidence and a smile. He went on to explain how it was comforting to know that there is a force greater than him. The first time he said it, I did not say anything, but by the third time, I could not help myself.

"There's nothing greater than you. There is no hierarchy."

I posed him a few questions about his experience with traditional medicine and discovered that he also did mushrooms. Though I cannot say word for word what he said about them, he made me curious when he briefly spoke about the universe. He explained how mushrooms are found on other planets such as Mars.

"It's universal."

It was then that I decided to make a mental note to research it and perhaps try it.

Later that evening, I met another young man. He was from England. He asked me to set up an Ayahuasca retreat for him through my shaman. I agreed and left him.

Friday, July 22, 2011:

Morning found my new friend Joe and I in the Amazon jungle with Esther, her older sister, their parents, and later in the afternoon don Herberto. Joe wanted to try only two sessions of Ayahuasca because of his time constant.

We started the session at about half past eight in the evening. I did not take any, for I was there to assist him. Don Herberto only gave him two doses, but boy was he a lot of work for us. I have to say that I am laughing now as I write because he was totally in the spirit realm. He mumbled things out about his mother, family, a girl, and all the while kicking his feet about and trying to dig his fist into his mouth. Esther went to comfort him by holding his head on her thigh like a baby. I held his left hand and don Herberto did his shamanic prayers and dance. He vomited like there is no tomorrow. All throughout this, I kept telling him to focus on the purest part of his Light. When he started calming down, he repeated what I was telling him, "The light, nothing can touch you."

Morning would find him rejuvenated and thankful. He explained that he saw us from far, far away, and that to him we were Gods trying to help him. He would also explain that he kept digging his hands into his mouth to get rid of a big snake.

The ensuing day Joe had a second intake of the Ayahuasca medicine, but this time don Herberto only gave him a dose. I also took a dose myself, hoping to get rid of the rest of the palpitations that I had been feeling since I went to Iquitos. Unfortunately, this did not help. As a result, I stopped don Herberto in front of my casita to ask him about the remaining palpitations in my body.

"How long before the palpitations in my body disappear?"

"About three to four weeks."

"And if they don't disappear?"

"The important thing is that you're protected by Ayahuasca."

My eyebrows and my forehead rose as if to say that he had given me an unsatisfactory answer, but I knew when to stop beating a dead horse.

"I have palpitations too. It comes with the job we do. It can't harm me."

After listening to Herberto, I thought there were two things for me to do. The first was to wait until the four-week period was over to see if he was right. The second was to turn to my second original plan: Peyote. I understood that it provides spiritual protection, and was confident that it would resolve the rest of my problems.

July 23, 2007:

I was in my bungalow, next to the door by a portable mirror hanging on a nail to the right of the door's threshold. I paused there in the darkness as a 2009 memory came back to me with clarity. The recollection of my soul vehemently arguing with my father in Light spirit form appeared sharply photographically. My mind clearly recalled observing its Light Self. Even as I brood over it now, I still cannot recall why my Light Self was so intensely arguing with him. Both sides were sternly set and unmovable. It was like two impenetrable, solid mountains.

I walked back slowly and pensively to my bed, feeling like a fool. The feeling that there are layers of each person came to me again, and I felt like a baby, a child left out. I understood that evening that the mind can be a stranger to the soul, for it keeps most of its memories hidden.

When I got under the covers, another piece of memory came to me. I was residing on the third floor of my newly purchased house. I woke up one Saturday morning writing something on a piece of paper next to my right in the nearly empty room. It read something like:

"Every child needs a father."

I clearly remember crying when I woke up. This was strange, for I was not accustomed to crying.

I understood that both recollections were linked, connected.

A third wave of memory came to me. I found myself at the capital as a little child. My mother was standing close to the entrance of the door. I watched my father and mother exchange words. My father handed me some money.

"Go buy some matches."

I understood him without a shadow of a doubt, though I was very young. I walked outside. The street seemed infinite, surreal, but magically beautiful and wondrous. This was undoubtedly fantastic though I would later be unable to make the connection to who I really am.

Later I would verify this story with my mother as I sat on a bench surrounded by several trees in my apartment complex.

"Tell me about the time you guys were arguing in the apartment where he asked me to go buy matches."

"Agbessi!" my mother would exclaim in surprise, "You were only two years old."

"It feels like yesterday. And walking on the streets felt magical, light. He wanted to burn your things!...

"I returned to the house, handing him the matches. The next thing I recalled were flames rising in a garbage can. Maybe I was closer to three?"

"You were two!" she insisted.

I found it incredulous that a two-year would be able to go out to the front of the house and actually purchase matches, but I was not going to dwell on that.

Morning found me getting ready to depart El Mundo Mágico and reflecting, always reflecting. The image of the vision that I had before coming to Peru kept coming to me.

Could it be possible? But, I can't think of any other explanations. The knowing smile. 'I'll meet you down there.' No, it could not be anyone else. It was indeed Mother Ayahuasca who appeared in my vision to guide me to the jungle.

CHAPTER 9

HEALING OLD WOUNDS

About a week after returning from my trip, amazing, flabbergasting things started happening that would erase any doubt that don Herberto had indeed been attacked by "the man with the two headed snake."

I engaged in several spiritual combats. In my first one, I found myself in a room full of black magicians or "sorcerers" as some people might call them. They were all black men, African, so it appeared. I was standing up, while they were sitting. The one to my left in the back stood up, and the battle began. He sent forward waves or thoughts of light dark energy to strike me. I stopped them by blowing out concentrated breaths of air—a technique I had unconsciously acquired through the Ayahuasca ceremonies. He, in turn, blocked my breath of energy that I casted forward at him.

The rest of the magicians rose against me, casting their spells simultaneously. Though, I was able to block them all, I found them to be formidable opponents.

The scene changed to a room where I was talking to a slim West African girl…I turned over in my bed but did not awake. I went outside. There was a little figure of some sort of vase, which I instinctively knew was concealing a magician. I broke it on the ground. The initial sorcerer came outside to continue the fight. He was very skilled at blocking my rays of none physical energy. Before I knew it, I woke up with a sore hand.

The week that ensued was even more fascinating. More sorcerers came after me in the so-called "dream" state. I found myself in a house that comprised a large room and a kitchen. There was a young child to my right. The sorcerer was trying to enter through the main door. I put the child behind me. Somehow, the sorcerer got into the house. I looked at him patiently, trying to decide what source of weapon to use—fire within my hand, wind, or storm? I started with the wind and blew him back into the abyss. He was thrown against the wall; the door opened and he went out flying. Then, I reinforced this blow with a storm, then I held fire in my hand, ready to employ it. But, I did not need it. I closed the door.

"Wow!" I said, waking up, "That's what I am talking about!"

Once again, my hands were sore. I knew then that these events had indeed taken place, but in a different realm of existence.

In September of 2011, I found myself combating demons again—shadows to be precise. A preadolescent girl was with me. She brought me a cell phone. She threw it on the floor. Noise emanated from it. The shadow demons surrounded the bed. I blew them away one by one with my breath. The girl stood by my left side as we watched the bed in calm. I called my mother in the evening.

"Did Akofa have a weird dream today?"

She said she did not know and went to get my sister for me.

"So, did you have a weird dream today?"

"I have weird dreams all the time," Akofa answered.

"Do you remember any in particular?"

She explained, but it did not match my own dream. This dream was so real that I call it "an altered reality experience." I decided to wait to see if it would prove to be more than a dream.

A few days after the above spiritual combat with the sorcerers, several conversations that I had with my mother kept replaying in my mind. The first occurred when I was driving on a local suburban area in the State of New York, when I called her.

"Don't forget to find the D.A.'s phone number for me," I told her.

She was disturbed.

"What do you want his number for?"

"The visit."

"You can't change a killer," she pronounced with heaviness and pain in her voice.

A few minutes later, Messa called me to inquire about my conversation with Dada. She had told him about my intention to visit my stepfather in California, and apparently she thought I was betraying her. This was according to Messa.

A few days later, the conversation resumed while I was driving again.

"He's a killer! You can't change him."

"I don't want to change him. I'm just passing on a message."

I drove, thinking about why I wanted to visit my stepfather. I had several reasons for going. First, my brother came to mind. I thought that maybe going could bring

Essevi peace, for I knew that he would go with me. Furthermore, I wanted to pass on the ultimate God-message, and to help my stepfather remember who he really is beyond the physical body, and to give him the chance to seek the Light sooner than later. Though the above reasons were indeed true, deep inside, I think the real reason was because of the firm intent that I sent to the Universe to heal my old wounds using the law of attraction. In such pursuit, I booked a flight to California for late August of 2011.

Friday, August 26, 2011:

On Friday morning, I took the train and a bus to the prison where Avon was supposed to be. Unfortunately, I learned that he was not there and was told to go to a different location, near Sacramento. I was a little disappointed, but I was at least fortunate to have gotten a ride from an office which was connected to the prison system.

There I was in the passenger's seat going back to the greyhound bus station. We were speaking Spanish. I was holding back on how much to share. She, on the other hand, seemed very relaxed and calm.

"My brother died years back. I had a dream of him. He seemed alright."

"It sounds like he came to say goodbye," I said.

"You're a very good person. Your stepfather killed your brother and you're here to help him," she said with a hint of a smile and serenity. Thitherto, I had been staring at a haze, straight ahead as I spoke. Now, however, my eyes jolted to my left. I was staring at this Hispanic woman. I could not remember being specific about her declaration. I was pretty sure I didn't tell her that my stepfather had killed my brother, so how did she know? I was dumfounded.

"I must have told her without paying attention," I tried to reassure myself, *"Perhaps she deduced it."*

Sunday, August 28, 2011:

Today, I experienced the reinforcement of a very important lesson: The hardest battle is within the self. After nearly eighteen years of listening to my mother express her pain and sorrow for my brother Essevi's death, I came to the stark realization that she intends to hold onto the guilt of losing him as long as she could. As I sat across from her in the kitchen, it was evident to me that this pain would stay with her into her next incarnation.

"The more you hold onto it, the more likely you are to attract similar negative situations. It's the law of attraction. By holding onto the pain you're making yourself weaker."

Her face pinched with pain and anger, my mother leaned forward slightly, and launched a few bad words into the air. I quickly stopped her with a wave of the hand.

"No, this is negative energy. I cannot be part of this any longer. I made a promise to myself."

"I have to let it out."

"Then you'll do it without the bad words."

"Do you want me to rise or drown?"

"What do you think I want?" I replied.

"I think you want me to rise."

"I am listening."

Minutes passed as I listened to her express her pain, trying to find an opening, a chance to say something new to have her *really* listen, but I found myself repeating the same thing that I have been telling her for eighteen years. Finally, I thought of a new approach.

"He's possessed."

"A demon!"

"Yes."

"He was influenced," she said as if thinking.

I do not recall the exact words that ensued from her mouth, but I do remember her saying something to the effect of not being able to accept the fact that there is something that made him less guilty.

I stopped to consider her words. I was aware that most people in the world would think that the word "possession" automatically means "control of the possessed person's mental processes." From my own personal experience, I did not find this to be true. The negative beings that were in my physical vehicle were cohabitating my body. As I explained earlier in this book, it was the depression and negative feelings that came with the radiation (i.e., the vibration) of their negative energy in my body that manifested themselves as signs of their "control."

The other negative effect with the cohabitation, as I alluded to before during my last Ayahuasca intake, was the impediments in recovering all of my visions.

I returned my thoughts to my mother.

"Oh, he's absolutely guilty alright. No one can ever make you do anything. Entity possession works in different ways. They cannot control you if your Light is bright."

"I feel so violated," she said.

"I feel violated too. These entities were inside of…" I said, then stopping suddenly.

"There are things that are not talked about…He manipulated me…He's doing that now. He's trying to get out of prison…Your brother, he knew. I did not listen and he took him from me. Your brother knew. He threatened me. He said, 'If you have the baby I'll take something precious away from you...'"

"I know, you've told me before," I said, thinking that we were not on the path that I had intended.

I wanted to go back to the reason why I brought up the demonic entity, but my mother was very deep into the "gun incidents."

I learned from her that Avon had actually taken a gun to two trips they went on while they were married. One was Lake Tahoe, in California, while the other was when they went to Chicago. I definitely did not remember her telling me about the latter.

"He actually took a gun with him?" I asked.

"He told me to stay in the car, and if anything happens to drive off right away. He did not want me to meet his family…He said his brother lived on the second floor, which didn't have any stairs…The place was like a war zone!" she said with a countenance of utter disbelief.

Presently, it was Monday evening. My mother and I sat in the kitchen. She sat in the side closest to the blinds. We were talking about not being able to see Avon. I thought I had taken much notes, I did not remember exactly how the conversation commenced. I only recall my mother saying:

"He came to my room….he cried."

"After the deed was done?" I asked, slightly astonished. She was talking about Avon returning to her and crying after killing Essevi. At that very moment, I wanted to cry, not because I was sad or that I lost my brother, but because I was again witnessing the overall message of Infinity. I lowered my eyes. Memories of the Ayahuasca session came back to me: "*A flicker of Light, is it always enough?*"

I was happy inside, crying, trying not to let my mother see it. I turned to control myself.

"We have much work to do. I've seen much, much worse—a world so sickening that I didn't want to endure it even for a moment.'

"I have seen beings that make Avon look like an angel."

"I'm an angel compared to Avon," my mother retorted.

I had gotten up, standing by the refrigerator, overcome by an overwhelming intuitive, emotional state. My heart was rendered to a melody of emotional suppleness and I felt like weeping again. I turned my eyes from my mother and offered her silence.

"He can do it," I said inside my head. For the life of me, my mind could not understand how these intuitive emotions were dawning on me.

I turned my body and my attention back to her.

"He was downstairs," my mother said.

At that time, I was sleeping downstairs in Avon's old room.

"He was downstairs!" my mother repeated with a stern, firm and serious countenance. She seemed absolutely sure.

I stared at her. My mind took a detour in memory lane. I exited my room, hearing the house alarm, knowing full well that something terrible had just transpired. The alarm was going off—I suddenly snapped out of it, sort of. I was looking at my mother, but my mind was still back in the old house. Avon had told my brother Messa to go take out the trash, and the house alarm was off then.

This made total sense, *for how could he have had a conversation with my mother and my younger brother without any noise if the alarm had not been initially turned off?"*

"He came downstairs first to try to take me out?" I asked.

Her countenance depicted a definite "yes."

"You're refusing to let go of the past," I said to her.

What would come out of her mouth next would be something I knew to be true that I would also hear from one of my students.

"You can't change anyone. Only they can change themselves."

"You're right," I said, walking to my temporary room as I stared down the floor with a smile, "We're *all* free. There's more than one way to skin a cat."

This statement was pretty much to let her know unconsciously that I would never give up on her, though I may have to resort to tough love.

Later that evening at about 6 p.m., my mother was watching the news which brought her back to her determined state of not letting go. The news program had given to a movie preview about revenge.

"That's right!" she exclaimed with her brows gathered into a frown.

I really did not know what was happening that day, but the series of topics that were presenting themselves before us seemed to be more than a coincidence to me. I thought about the law of attraction. The news program came on again, this time the topic was about the death penalty. I used to be a supporter of it. This was on principal, not in practicality. I thought it was better for the person to suffer in prison than to be killed, because death to me at that time was so final. I was mostly convinced that once the person died then that was it; and this did not make much sense to me. However, as I sat in my mother's couch in the living room, which lent itself to the swimming pool to my right, I knew that the death penalty was utterly futile. You cannot kill a soul. The soul will always survive no matter what.

What the government and society are doing then is to take away that person's chance to learn (e.g., to suffer or to cry). Each incarnation into the physical form takes a lot of planning and coordination. Part of Infinity along with the soul that would be born decided this together before birth. And so, when a life is ended prematurely, it slows down the Infinite Plan, which I described in my first book A Glimpse of Who We Are. This is because no matter how dark or bright our Lights, we are all connected. Race, religions, cultures, sex, gender, and so forth are all temporary experiences.

Two or three days later, I completely became aware of the differences between a dream, spiritual travel, and a spiritual message. I was on the plane back to New York. The window shade was open. The sun rejuvenated my eyes. I put the hood of my black jacket over my face to get some shut-eye. A few minutes later, a tall, beautiful girl with long, straight hair appeared before me.

"Please!" I said, contorting my face in disagreement. I knew what she came to do, so I shut her down by opening my eyes. It was my ex-girlfriend in Mexico. I knew immediately that this was no dream—it was a spiritual visit in her Light form. She herself was not psychic, but the soul has its own plans. I was happy, for I was finally able to decipher the difference between a dream and a spiritual visit.

Images of Hawa, my former "fiancée" in Togo also came to me. I was in front of my first grade classroom in Kusuntu, Togo. This was the school in which I used to wander and play when I was a child. I was wearing a tank-top in the vision. Hawa approached with a knowing smile. She told me in indirect words that she wanted to overlook the spells she had casted on me.

"It's ok. It's over," she said

I turned away from her, disgusted. It was not over, for even as I write now I still have things in me.

CHAPTER 10

STOPPING THE WORLD

Identity is a very powerful way of seeing and perceiving who we are. We human and none human beings identify with a lot of things. These things thus define and limit who we are. We identify with our race (i.e., being Black, White, Japanese, etc), profession (i.e., a police officer, a teacher), culture, religion (i.e., being Jewish, Buddhist, Christian, etc), sex (i.e., being male versus being female), being a fearful person, a homosexual, a heterosexual, a Republican, a Democrat and so forth. It is such temporary association with external factors that holds us in a state of static perception, a false identity and religion. It keeps us in a state of slavery.

After my spiritual combats, I made a firm promise —to stop the world. In order to do this, I decided to disassociate from all false or none long-lasting belief systems and actions that bind me to the ephemeral. Such disassociation would allow me to expand my global awareness so that I would not be limited to a static perception of the things around me, of all that is possible. By doing this, I would allow my senses to perceive what I could not before. As such, I knew I would no longer tolerate nonsense, abuse, or lies wherever it came from. In short, to stand up for myself and others.

In pursuit of expanding my identity and perception, I began using the law of attraction fifteen to sixteen hours a day. I used it while driving, walking alone or with others, while sleeping, at meetings, and especially while at work.

I used the law of attraction so habitually that my sense of sight literally began to expand. This occurred when we interviewed for the French Beginning 2 post, which lasted for two days. During the first day of the interviews, I sat very close to my boss Kathy. I felt a very strong discomfort of fear and rumbling literally in my stomach, which mounted up my chest. For the life of me I could not understand why this was happening. This negative feeling was definitely not about my disagreement with my boss manipulating my teaching schedule. I thought about the negative entities in my body. The mere thought of this seemed to have halted the feeling.

During the second set of interviews, the bizarre feeling that I experienced before was gone. However, the nature of my awareness was about to change forever. My boss Kathy was sitting directly across from me, to her left was a parent—helping us with the interview. I stared right into her eyes to understand how she could be screwing with me like this. I focused on her eyes. My eyes were glued upon hers. Suddenly, my mind was blown back. I leaned back in my chair, my eyes paralyzed in an immobility of a daze.

"No way!"

Her eyelids fluttered and closed in a slow movement like George Bush the father.

"This woman is not a benign alien species. She herself is probably not aware of it. Interesting!

We were now interviewing another person.

His command of the French language was not that good.

I kept an eye on the movements of my boss's eyelids.

Most of his answers were tautological. It wasn't because he was nervous. He was not prepared, and his French was quite rusty.

"...Her French was quite good. There might be some problems with the schedule; she wanted something in the evening," my boss said.

September 6, 2011:

Today was the day I began *to stop* the world. Like the previous years, she had given me too many preparations.

At 3:22 p.m., I sent an e-mail to my boss Kathy about my teaching schedule. It read:

> I came in today to begin preparing for the ensuing academic year and decided to look at my teaching schedule and class lists. There are several problems with them. The AP French 5 roster only has one student listed. In terms of AP French 4, ...and...should be in AP4 if the schedule permits. They were initially recommended for this course.

> In addition, my teaching schedule indicates that I am teaching three French 3H courses. In June of 2011 when the three of us met to speak about the schedule and my concerns about the excess of preparations I have been teaching since I was hired, the schedules you showed us clearly indicated two French 3R classes. Now, the names have been changed from "R" to honors. I strongly anticipate a few major problems with this. I strongly believe that such a change in appellation will be evident to the students. The AP French 4 the ensuing 2012-2013 academic year will be a complete disaster because they will not be ready to handle the rigors of the advanced placement course. It will lower their confidence in us and the French program, and probably the school.

The above e-mail was "cc-ed" to the assistant principal Melissa. Melissa first responded with:

> There were 11 requests for the AP French 5. I was only able to get 7 in the class at the time. I don't know why only one was scheduled. The other four students will speak to their counselor next week. As you know, the students taking all upper level courses usually have to make difficult decisions with their classes…

Melissa did not say anything about the alterations with the change in name in terms of the French 3 classes. She was responsible for the scheduling, not Kathy the principal.

On Tuesday, September 6, 2011 at 8:03 a.m. Kathy answered:

> The curriculum for French 3 and 3H is the same, except for more 3H writing assignments, from what I remember when I wrote it. Our students will only benefit from the added rigor as they prepare for college and career. I'm confident that you will help them meet the challenge.
>
> Kathy

On Tuesday, September 6, 2011, 1:40 p.m. I spoke to my foreign language union representative about the situation, for I knew Kathy had no intention to do the right thing by properly aligning the courses. After meeting with her, I sent the head union person of the building the following e-mail:

> Hello Bill, the bottom part of the e-mail is what I sent Kathy on Friday when I came to start preparing my classroom: 160. Last Thursday Dona and I, a parent, and the Principal interviewed two teachers for the French Beg.2 class. I bring this up because there is a 0.2 French Beg.2 class position at Spring Valley, and 0.4 French Beg.2 class at the other high school. Playing with this would have give me three preps instead of the current situation. Keep in mind that Kathy has been doing this since I got here. She's the one who has approved the schedule every single time. This is the sixth year.
>
> Agbe

Wednesday, September 7, 2011: Day 1 of classes:

Today was the first day of classes. I found myself in the foreign language office with a colleague.

"I am glad you stood up for yourself."

"Yeah, it's an absolute nonsense what she's doing."

"She had the opportunity to give you a fair schedule, but she didn't to keep herself looking good because of your highs scores," he said to my surprise.

"So you understand more than I thought. I don't think she understands who she's really up against. This awakened soul is making his stand. Bullshit days of old are gone."

I became aware of two important things this month. The first deals with an unconscious memory trying to surface to the conscious: an ancient memory of who I once was. In pursuit of this expanded awareness, I finally bought From Elsewhere, a book I had been meaning to read for a while. Finally, in early October of 2011, I began reading it. Before I say what I am about to say, let me first preface it with the fact that I have never cried reading a book in my life. As I read it, however, I cried at least four times. I could no longer deny the obvious: This was not the only dimension or planetary system I have been in. A palpable realization of this acceptance began with my soul exiting its body in 2009 to defend its conscious self. As I have stated earlier, my soul spoke a language which I have yet to come across on this planet.

"But I don't feel like an alien," I heard myself say once as I read the book.

"What does it mean to be an extraterrestrial being from another planet or galaxy?"

Nothing! Everything is a distraction. Only the luminosity of the Light is constant.

Yet, upon the acceptance of this, I have had a hard time being limited to just one culture. Culture, religion, and our fake science put me in a very uncomfortable box.

The other important realization deals with the dyslexia I have had since high school. I cannot remember precisely when the "illness" began. I was teaching my third period class when it hit me like lightening. It was during my AP 5 French course. The students and I were reading The Little Prince. I turned to the black board.

"It's the same word in English," I said in French, "Enigma," I said and wrote on the board.

Then I faced my five students. I paused momentarily.

"Does it have an 'a'?"

They were not sure. "In any case, it means 'a mystery.' Something that eludes…We can check the spelling later. It's a cognate."

At that instant, it was absolutely clear to me what was transpiring. I felt a slight movement of a demon inside my left and right temples. This was the same "movement" I felt during the Ayahuasca health treatment. Speculation was no longer necessary—my intelligence or access to total awareness to a lesser extent was still being blocked. Nevertheless, I knew my Light pushed me on.

The ensuing day at about 7:12 or 7:13 am I began to recall countless times when I could not remember or felt out of my element. I was able to trace the demons' cohabitation in my body as early as my high school years. I counted at least seventeen years that some of them have been in my body.

Saturday, September 24, 2011:

I was driving to see a young comedian. He had given me a flyer several weeks thither. As I made a right turn on a road on which I often travelled to get to work, I was literally overcome with a strong feeling of uncertainty.

"How will all this work out?"

My mind wanted to know how my decision to stay the course with the publication of my first book and sharing what I know about the nature of existence play out. A recent vision that I had of juggling two worlds with ease flashed before my mind's eye as I drove alone. My mind was not at ease.

"I will protect you!" I heard my soul telling my mind.

"No!" I wailed out.

A week and a half later, this quasi-weak voice would thunder out:

"It's my turn. I trust you now. Despite the lack of uncertainty, I will be my own savior, I will follow you."

Successfully juggling two worlds? Incredible!

Thursday Morning, September 29, 2011:

Today, I asked myself if there were a connection between a vision that I had during the summer of 2011 and my attempted trip to San Luis Potosi, Mexico for my Peyote spiritual healing.

The vision transpired either on a Friday or a Saturday. I was on the left side of my big bed. My eyes closed, I was facing the head of the bed. I entered some sort of circular portal—my mind becoming lighter and lighter till there was total clarity, vividness of color. I was above the earth, a quasi-weightlessness—I seemed to have been everywhere as my Light body spread itself out. I shrunk myself and lowered my Light form. What was awesome about this was that I was everywhere within the entire planet simultaneously. I saw the planet being alive—having an essence, a Light form or a soul if you wish. All this transpired without needing a visa from Mother Earth. Then I lowered my Light being and grasped the physical soil within my hand. I was on a certain part of the planet where there was a lot of sand. It was vivid, tangible and almost surreal. I felt I was definitely not dreaming. I had travelled somewhere to communicate with Mother Earth.

The thing that astounded me the most was the lack of rules and restrictions one normally finds within the physical authorities of the Earth. They were totally absent. I needed no rules because I came to understand, for healing, in peace, without violence or abuse. Such love, such generosity—I found only with my brother Essevi, my father, and Mother Ayahuasca. I was impressed with Mother Earth. From that moment, I knew she is a beautiful being and I would never forget as I carried on with my own battles with the dark beings in my body.

Thursday afternoon, September 29, 2011:

I arrived at LaGuardia Airport about an hour and a half before my departure. I wrote as I waited. This activity quickly came to a halt when my eyes seized an officer in uniform. It was quite curious—the movement of his eyes! Not only was this 30-something year-old Hispanic man's eye lids flapping over his eyes completely, they were also blinking rather fast. I turned to another Hispanic—a very pretty woman. Her eyes did not flap or flicker that much. I was definitely onto something. There was another police officer who walked toward him. I focused on him. Though he was Caucasian, his eyes also flickered in the same manner as the Hispanic man. *So, some people are automatically drawn to certain occupations because of the nature of their species. These two police officers are definitely different species of the human race.* I figured they like to be in authoritative positions. I myself never cared for authoritative figures. For the most part, I used to feel that those at the very top were pretending to be more than they really are, when they are in fact really insecure inside.

My mind shifted to recalls of lucid moving images of me observing one of my students' eyes. The eyes never lie. He had slit eyes as that of a reptile. I could no longer deny that there are different species of human beings engineered or modified by a highly technologically advanced extraterrestrial race. The question that remained for me was: which alien group or groups is or are responsible for the dumbing down of the human race? Later, nearly after completing this book, further intuitive proofs would come to me.

I looked at the clock. It was about 1:25 p.m. I checked in and went through the security clearance. When I arrived at the gate area, I was told that my flight to the San Luis Potosi was delayed an hour: from 2:30 to 3:30 p.m. The time passed and the plane did not come. I went to talk to a tall, slender black lady at the counter, who said that the plane would come at 5:30 p.m. That was another three hours away. By this time, I was not convinced the plane was coming at all.

"Is this fate or really just a weather problem," I said rhetorically. I asked for a refund and was on my way back to New York City. On my way back I called my mother and related the incident to her.

"Maybe they're protecting you," she said.

I took the "they" to mean my brother, father and Mother Ayahuasca.

October 2011:

I think it is safe to say that some people do not trust politicians, and I would say with good reason. I would also add that most overly rich people are often not pure of heart. You see, I have wondered for a long time what Bill Gates was really doing to change the world with his billions of dollars. I mean give me $400,000 and you'll see what I can do in the continent of Africa.

I typed in the name Bill Gates and clicked on "videos." I watched his eyes as he spoke on the telescreen. He was on a computer screen and a lot of people including young children were gazing at him like a hero. They were attentively listening to him. My eyes were fixed on his.

"This guy knows secrets! No wonder he's rich. he's not a genius."

I took a deep breath.

I am not in Kansas anymore, am I?

I was on a role and wanted to check out a few other people. I typed *Ron Paul* on the computer. This was a man, a politician who actually told the truth. He spoke publicly about how money is not real—how it is printed out of thin air, how the Federal Reserve system is really a private institution controlled by global bankers. I have also listened attentively as he spoke about how Barack Obama should have refused the Nobel Peace prize. As I watched, I clicked other videos—close ups; and again—the fluttering of his eyes was curious. I clicked on another video where he was being posed questions about the dismantling of the Federal Reserve system. When he hesitated about how fast the system can change, I knew he was hedging. *Shades of grey!* The control system is brilliant. There are those in great position of power such as Rosh Limbaugh, senators and presidents who straight out lie about their true intentions. The Bush family is more or less obvious. Obama uses sweet words and then drops bombs on countries. Still yet, others are slick like the fox. Foxes are more formidable. What they do is tell us 70, maybe 80 percent of the truth. This is where the brilliancy comes in. The control system gives us an array of deception, which goes from evil to clouded lightness, hoping to keep us trapped within this prison planet.

The time is now about 6 p.m. As I graded my French AP 4 students' subjunctive assignments while listening to JFK's conspiracy speech, ideas were flowing into my mind. They were flowing in forms of moving pictures. I saw myself making a video, speaking about how Obama intended to take us more into the darkness. I typed in his name onto Google video search. A thought came to me about Ron Paul. Advertisements about his 2012 presidential bid appeared. Finally, my long awaited search, quest was over. Ron Paul was being interviewed by someone about September 11. I wondered how someone like him who knew so much about how the system is manipulating us not know that George Bush could not have seen the first plane hit the Twin Towers. It was at that moment when I knew without a shadow of a doubt that my Ayahuasca experience about the political system being a distraction is absolutely accurate. There is no one safe to vote for. Ron Paul would not help dismantle the control system.

Friday, October 7, 2011:

Today, my battle against *stopping* the world took a twist. It began at about 8:45 in the morning when I said:

"Hello officer."

He returned my hello. I did not remember my exact words to him, but I literally leaned back at his answer.

"That's bull-shit!"

I knew immediately that he was speaking from his controlled mind, and not his soul. He was blind like billions of souls because of his spiritual manipulation beyond the limited five senses.

"Where are you from?" he asked the tall brown girl standing to his left next to the door.

"The Dominican Republic," the student answered.

"See? There! You're in denial!" he said with force.

I looked at my blind colleague with a mixture of sadness and disconcertedness. Perchance, it was this sincere frankness or perhaps not, but his right hand went up and he said something to the effect of "You know I love you man" as we pounded our fists. The phone rang.

"See? I have friends!"

I waited a few seconds and left. As I walked toward the foreign language office, I thought about my failure *to stop* my mind.

"Why did you even go there?" I asked myself.

I entered the foreign language office.

"That was a waste of time. You knew he's blind, a sleeping beauty indulging in the superficiality of existence. Patience Agbessi! How long did it take you to remember your eternity?"

Saturday, October 8, 2011:

We were in a quasi-empty parking lot. A cop drove by to the north of us. I was giving driving lessons to Kevin who was sixteen years old: a tall, young black adolescent. It was his first time driving. I was sitting on the passenger seat. To our left was the cop again driving toward us. I was looking right at him. His eyes seemed to be telling me that he wanted to talk to us.

"Stop, Kevin!" I said twice.

Kevin had not quite mastered his “response time” yet. That is, he did not quite know how to stop the car in a timely manner when asked.

The curious thing was that a strange feeling of fear vibrated in my left chest area. I knew immediately what was happening. One of the several remaining demons inside of me was afraid.

The cop! Authority! Power! I do not bow down to authority, so why was I feeling this way? Suddenly, I had it with utter clarity. This was the second time I recognized and did not identify with the fear. To me, this was great, for despite my setbacks. This was yet another step forward to augmenting my awareness and stopping the world. The cop leaned his head out of the car.

“You’re practicing?” he asked nicely.

“Yes,” Kevin replied, and the cop left.

The incident made me think of my Ayahuasca experience in Peru. These demons followed rules. They fear authority. Their society is structured on hierarchy and immense fear of consequences.

Today, I saw a colleague I had been looking for *for* two weeks. She had promised to buy me some *wormwood*, an organic liquid extract detox medicine to get out toxins such as worms in the body. Kimberly began with:

“So, where are you from?”

“God, the Universe,” I said with a smile.

“Are you an Islander?...”

“No, seriously I am from God,” I said.

“See, I get it. I am spiritual,” she said, as if reading my mind.

"Well, some people can't handle it," I said, pointing to the police officer's door, "No other identity will do. I looked for you," I said to Kimberly, "but I could not find you."

"That's because I was at the other school for the last two weeks."

"How many of the wormwood did you buy?"

"Ten."

I was hoping she would say that she had some for me. She did not bring them. I sensed she did not want to give me any. In any case, I did not wait for her. I had bought my own a couple of days before seeing her. I told her this.

"So what happened when you took it?" Kimberly asked me.

"I felt heat in certain parts of my body and chest area."

"Nothing on the skin or when you used the bathroom?"

"No, but I remember you telling me that something dried up on your skin."

She paused to clarify.

"We all have parasites in our bodies."

I knew she was right, but a few months later, my mind would be blown open to the depth of the accuracy of her statements.

"Then you don't have worms. They're parasites."

"What do you have?" she asked in wonder.

"I'll tell you little by little as not to scare you.

The time was now at 3:51 p.m. After writing notes in my journal, I came to the conclusion that even now I was still a bit harsh on myself. I understood that I have made much progress in *stopping* myself. This morning, I felt low energy. I was immediately aware of the fact that it was not me.

Between 10-11:40 a.m. I was cooking cabbage tomato soup as I created scenarios inside my head about how to have better dealt with my school police officer colleague. For an hour and a half, I reenacted Friday's scenario in my head. I kept failing. I saw my mind holding to some form of "explanation." That is, my mind kept explaining itself to the police officer. My mind again was trying to hold onto its ego. This was a difficult battle. Every time I failed at *not doing*, I paused, took a *deep* breath and tried again. *The ego must go* if I am to become my ultimate Light Self.

"Stop being so stubborn!" I said as I sliced the onions. By 4 p.m. my mind surrendered completely to purity. I now had the calm feeling that I was successful at "not doing." This mainly involved not talking, not explaining myself to the sleeping blind when I sense it will have no positive effect on them.

"The law of attraction is always at work," I said as I entered the library.

Tuesday, October 11, 2011:

Today, I realized that the law of attraction was at work again. There are moments when you surrender to sexual and sensual ecstasy; and when it is happening, your private parts scream out for more.

I was sitting at my desk, in front of my desktop computer, listening to some Ewe music as I ate my quasi-vegan sandwich: It had muenster cheese. It was a simple sandwich, really. It contained onions, tomatoes, vegan protein slices and vegetarian mayonnaise. All of the ingredients were organic, of course. I took a bite off the right corner. I swallowed and breathed in with pleasure—a slow, deep exhalation of a slight moan. I took another bit. I swallowed slowly again, letting the exquisite feeling take over my throat, skipping my stomach and reaching or rather culminating in my *rod* with an eye-pooping "Oh! Ok!"

My mind was trying to figure out how this feeling could be happening. A part of me wanted to shut it down without hesitation—the body was in too much rapturous delight.

After the meal, I made a mental note: *My operation to shut down my mind was being more successful then I thought.*

I wanted to stump my left feet with joy, but something held the sensation for a few seconds. Then, it was over and I leaned back in my seat feeling a bit empty. Though I had enjoyed the experience, I did not understand this emptiness that I felt after the experience.

Later that Sunday, between 7-8 p.m. a big fly stormed into my bedroom. The door was open. The buzzing of the insect was startling.

"Where did you come from?"

I thought this was weird. I tried to swat it without killing him, but every time he evaded me and I could not bring him down. I did not like flies and wanted to get rid of it, but a soft voice challenged me *to see, to perceive* beyond the ephemeral.

About twenty minutes later, I was in the second room about to shave my face—my beard. As I turned right, the fly appeared again. I tried to swat at it without hitting it hard to subdue it, to take it outside—to set it free—to preserve the God within.

As I swatted at it, its noise ceased. I pondered its eternity, yet I could not hear Him. I left feeling a bit dejected. *Did I kill Him?* Before I knew it, the fly was back in my living room. *I have to send him out with calm, without destroying you.* The fly came to my face. My white shirt swung softly at him. He went into the next room.

Sunday, October 23, 2011:

I had my eyes closed, but I heard a voice to my right that was not of this world. I remained silent, thinking that perhaps it was not real—just a dream. I was slightly falling asleep. My thoughts took over, trying to find a rational explanation. The more I ignored the negative being, the louder his complaints and wailing became. I smiled and was about to open my eyes when I suddenly changed my mind. I thought it would be futile to try to see the monster with my physical eyes. I ignored him for deep inside, I knew he had no power over me. The only power he would have was what I offered him. He came closer to my bed, behind my head, making ugly faces. My mind's eyes (i.e., Third Eye) looked at him with indifference, a detached feeling. I turned over and tried to sleep, hoping to have a sweet, lucid dream.

Half an hour passed and sleep did not come. Still, I could not resign: I kept my eyes closed. Finally, I found myself in a somewhat open court area. To my left and my back where walls. I flapped my arms like a bird, taking off the ground and standing in mid-air. I shook my body as if trying to cast away the heaviness. I pushed by body forward as Superman would when flying. Though I moved in the air, there was stiffness and a heaviness about my body. I flew to my left, landing against the wall with my left foot in an extended position. I willed myself to cast away the demons inside my body, they were stubborn. Yet, my body was still very stiff. I felt a soft wave of thought: *To stop the mind*, you must pay attention to details. I knew then that what was happening was real. It was happening in another realm of perception and I was catching onto it. This was again another hint that I was trying to stop my mind even in the sleep state.

When I woke up, I turned in my bed for another half an hour and finally fell into another dream again. This time I found myself in my school's cafeteria in the kitchen area. A few students were buying food. I found myself feeling light—physically, very light. I began levitating—there was a light energy about me.

Later I found myself at the gym on the Tread Mill, running with my small earphones in my ears when I was suddenly struck by an invisible sharp object in the forehead. Since my Ayahuasca experience, my intuition has been sharpening.

October 23, 2011:

"Shades of grey" I found myself saying as I woke up on Sunday at 8:20 in the morning. Somehow, I found myself looking for the English version of the

Bible in the apartment. The French version was in my car and I did not feel like going outside for it. It took a few minutes, but I found it in the living room. I turned to Psalm 91. As I read, modifying the words, I found myself in the company of images of days of old—in my room. I smiled. *There was never any reason to have been afraid or worried in those days.* I read on. My eyes nearly popped out when I came to the words "You will not fear the terror of the night nor the arrow that flies by day." My voice ceased and silence overtook me and all thoughts halted for about two seconds. *The arrow! It's a literal arrow!*

Wednesday, October 26, 2011:

It appears to me that more and more public schools are built like prisons from inside and out. How many schools do you know in New York that have an open area that you can look up and see the sky? When I was going to school in California, we children exited our classrooms and stepped outside and walked upon the natural ground. If you don't understand what I am talking about yet, then I beg you to consider a university campus. The buildings are not built as a single enclosed unit. One goes from building to building and can actually see the open sky.

The physicality of the structure of public schools, to me is indicative of the chaos that brews inside the buildings. This chaos is a result of a monolithic destructive force. There is a religion that maintains this force. It is so powerful that it has created atheists, faltered enthusiastic truth seekers, encouraged students to read atheist or quasi-atheist books, kept students, teachers, parents and administrators in a vicious cycle of blaming each other. Its poison goes deep. It is routine and repetitive. It is quite formidable because its infiltration is ominous and nearly inescapable. This religion is called science, and its biggest subsidiary is the education system.

A few days have passed. Given the fact that there are no consequences for the children, student misbehavior has spiked at work. Compared to the previous year, there were more fights. Some teachers and well-behaved students were beginning to complain.

"Everyone pretends there's nothing wrong," my female foreign language colleague said.

"I definitely understand," I assured her, taking my eyes off my school notebook. I began taking notes on their conversation on the blue nurse's card that was sitting at my desk.

Later that day, I searched through my desk for the memo sent by the principal. I read it carefully. It did not have any names except the principal's signature. The letter read:

> …High School…To:
> Thank you for your support of the school administration, particularly the Student Management Office, in maintaining a positive school climate. I would like to emphasize the importance of collaboration in handling student issues and completing the disciplinary referral for the Student Management Office. If a potential threat to safety occurs and a student must be immediately removed from the classroom, please

fill out a referral subsequent to the removal and submit it on the same day. Otherwise, please follow the procedures explained below.

The Discipline Referral Form demonstrates the teamwork necessary to meet the emotional and behavioral challenges facing our students. The teacher is the leader in his or her classroom and in the majority of situations issues are handled by speaking to the student and then the parent. Those are the first and second steps in the referral process. If behavior disruptive to teaching and learning continues, the third step is to consult the chairperson or department supervisor. Their role is to support the teacher by providing techniques to incorporate into the classroom in order to manage the issues. Each department office has a copy of the Pre-Referral Intervention Manual, filled with strategies. If the strategies attempted do not have a positive impact, the school counselor should be notified. They often have valuable information to share with regard to outside factors impacting our students. If none of the above interventions proves successful, the completed referral should be submitted to the Student Management Office. This is the only point at which the referral needs to be submitted. On reverse is a sample referral for your information.

If you have any questions about this process, feel free to speak to any member of the school administration.

As soon as I read the correspondence, I understood its objective. During the staff meeting in the cafeteria at the beginning of the school year, the principal informed us that our school had not met the *No Child Left Behind NYP*. As a result, we were put on "a needs to improve" list. In an attempt to solve this problem, the school administration designed a new "discipline referral form."

At this juncture, I would like to share with you Reader a story that was given to me by one of my graduate teachers about a year ago that shows how confused even our education leaders are. It is called "The Hot Air Balloon":

A man in a hot air balloon realized he was lost. He reduced altitude and spotted a woman below. He descended a bit more and shouted:

"Excuse me, can you help me? I promised a friend I would meet him a while ago, but I don't know where I am."

The woman below replied, "You're in a hot air balloon hovering approximately 30 feet above the ground. You're between 40 and 41 degrees north latitude and between 59 and 60 degrees west longitude."

"You must be a teacher," said the balloonist.

"I am," replied the woman, "How did you know?"

"Well," answered the balloonist, "everything you told me is technically correct, but I've no idea what to make of your information, and the fact is I'm still lost. Frankly, you've not been much help at all. If anything, you've delayed my trip."

The woman below responded, "You must be a school administrator."

"I am," replied the balloonist, "but how did you know?"

"Well," said the woman, "you don't know where you are or where you're going. You have risen to where you are due to a large quantity of hot air. You made a promise, which you've no idea how to keep, and you expect people beneath you to solve your problems. The fact is you are in exactly the same position you were in before we met, but now, somehow, it's my fault."

Thursday, October 27, 2011:

Further proof that the religion of science has taken its roots and is destroying not only students' minds but also their souls, occurred for me when I was chatting with one of my students. She was asking questions about narcissists. We were discussing the film The Secret as it relates to the Law of Attraction.

"The other 1% relates to your life purpose: If it's not in your path, then no matter how much you concentrate on it or pray for it, it won't happen…Whatever you're working on, is what manifests—good or bad.

"Watch me!" I said, "Lightly poke your right eye with your index finger. What do you see?"

"A light," she answered.

"Good," I said, "There's a reason why the light is there."

A few days later, I would see her reading Nietzsche.

"You seem tired," I said to her.

She seemed to be in a daze: hypnotized from insufficient rest.

"I was never able to finish or even get much into it. It wasn't making any sense…It's unbelievable. You're already reading that in high school?"

She observed me with calm eyes.

"I have a book for you, to get another perspective on existence. I'll bring it for you tomorrow."

I left her in the science class and returned to my classroom.

Friday, October 28, 2011:

Two students rushed to me, asking why I called their houses. The first student who was to my right, near her locker insisted that I had called her house. I assured her that I had not. Then, she explained how the district's information had appeared on the monitor. I smiled.

"This is excellent news," I said.

Last year, the assistant principal at the Office of Student Management was trying to accomplish such a task—the district turned it down. Automatic phone calls to parents for tardy students. It was only under pressure that the district was willing to correct the problem. Reader, remember, the district still has the same monetary problem, it is only then that it was willing to act morally.

Later that morning, I walked into an office and overheard the ensuing conversation about the new discipline guideline.

"The discipline system is in response to the state."

I listened with total interest. I looked at the sheet again.

"Interesting," I said, observing, and pondering.

"It's to show the State that we're improving—"

"Artificially," I added to my female colleague's comment.

I was slightly taken aback. *Amazing!* I expected a little more from this assistant principal—to make her stand for moral integrity.

That same day in the evening at about 8:40 p.m., certainty took hold of me. My mind was back in my Harlem small studio. I was reading Mein Kempf by Adolf Hitler. Throughout the book, he kept saying that there were "so few among them." He was referring to people in the "Third World" such as countries in Africa, India, and so forth. Even back then my intuition told me that there was much more than meets the eyes with that statement Hitler made.

I brought my attention back to the present. As the hot water ran down my back, my eyes averted to the left broken curtain rod. The intuitive knowing was now absolute—Hitler was absolutely not "racist." He was a very dark soul, who had been reincarnated over and over again, masquerading as human. His objective was to bring down the positive consciousness of this planet. From what dark star system he originated, I knew not, but I was categorically certain that *the few* about whom he spoke were very dark souls just like him who were hiding in "minority" human race form in developing countries.

It also became clear to me that Hitler was in contact with dark entities because he was one of their descendants.

Sunday, October 31, 2011:

Today, I gave a copy of the book Many Lives, Many Masters to the student. I was a little apprehensive about doing it, for I thought perhaps there was a chance this might conflict with her family's religious views, especially if she started talking about it at home.

In the evening, I returned to Hitler's book Mein Kempf. "*So few among them?*" Gotcha! It's the undertones. One audience was blind—took it literally, *the other* read between the lines—the new me. *Genetic manipulation?* Hitler definitely did not originate on this planet. I flipped through the pages to find clues about him being part of the control system.

On page 185, he admits:

"…I had indulged in angry thoughts concerning my earthly pilgrimage, which, as it seemed to me, had begun too late…"

"Ha!" I said. He was being literal here.

The time is now 10:28 p.m. I turned to the inside cover of the book to find clues to his racist propaganda. Written in the inside cover were pages 1236, 134-135, 145+, and 284. I had written these pages years ago for further analyses, not knowing exactly why. I thought perhaps my unconscious was at work even then.

I turned to 134. On this page, I found the following sentences underlined:

> But it is equally true that Nature as such has not reserved this soil for the future possession of any particular nation or race; on the contrary, this soil exists for the people which possesses the force to take it and the industry to cultivate it…Nature knows no political boundaries. First she puts living creatures on this globe and watches the free play of forces. She then confers the master's right on her favorite child, the strongest in courage and industry.

Upon reading those words, my intuition screamed out "Hitler, you didn't write this book. Someone else wrote it for you."

He was definitely part of a secret organization that connects to the shadow people. Darwin's theory of evolution sketched upon my mind like a brilliant torch. I immediately knew there was a connection. Hitler was using a lie to justify murder and his "right to kill people" through "the survival of the fittest" nonsense.

I turned to page 151, which discusses the preservation of the species. *Who or whatever group of people wrote this book for Hitler was in with the intent to deceive those who could not be deceived through religion. They would deceive the none-religious through another religion that is more pernicious and violent than traditional religions—science!*

I turned to page 153:

Never yet has a state been founded by peaceful economic means, but always and exclusively by the instincts of preservation of the species—regardless whether these are found in the province of heroic virtue or of cunning craftiness…

This was more of Darwin's bullshit. As I read on, I found more evidence of this. On page 285, he exclaims, "The stronger must dominate and blend with the weaker." Recall what Hitler said about there being "only a few" in developing countries as I explain the following. Throughout the book, he talks about the bloodline of the Aryan people—mostly White. The bottom of page 661 reads:

> No more than another nation renounces of its own accord the pursuit of its impulse for the expansion of its power and way of life, but is compelled by outward circumstances or else succumbs to impotence due to the symptoms of old age, does the Jew break off his road to world dictatorship…He, too, will either be thrown back in world domination…But the impotence of nations, their own death from old age, arises from the abandonment of their blood purity.

Have you had enough yet Reader? Yes, no maybe? Let's beat the dead horse a little more. On page 296, Hitler states:

> The Aryan gave up the purity of his blood and, therefore, lost his sojourn in the paradise which he had made for himself. He became submerged in the racial mixture, and gradually, more and more, lost his cultural capacity….Blood mixture and the resultant drop in the racial level is the sole cause of the dying out of the old cultures; for men do not

> perish as a result of that force of resistance which is contained in pure blood.

To me, Mein Kempf was a deliberate, intentional manufacture of hatred and racism. It is an extension of the false religion put forward through Charles Darwin's theory of evolution. I went extensively into detail about Hitler because a bit of research and awareness reveals that there are still many Hitlers among us all over the world.

Wednesday, November 2, 2011:

It was about 7 in the morning. The weather was bearable. I thought about how I used to identify with these demons. This time, however, I was totally aware of the fact that this was not me. They were separate entities within me that I intended to remove for good.

As I walked out of my apartment and mounted up the few stairs, I immediately felt nausea mostly within my chest and stomach area. I opened the car door. The nausea remained. I turned the engine on to warm up the car. I took out a little implement to scrape off the thin ice of the windshield and windows.

Thursday, November 3, 2011:

During the last American presidential elections, I had a couple of discussions with one of my ESL/Foreign language colleagues about the so-called 2008 "historic elections."

An image of her walking toward the right side of the 90s hallway left an indelible image in my mind's eye. A few minutes thither she had been arguing for Hilary Clinton, and I for Barack Obama.

Today, the thought came to me to ask her about her election choice.

"Who did you vote for in the 2008 presidential election?"

"We went to the polls…I just couldn't…"

I was fairly certain that she would have voted if Hilary had been the nominee. I understood that she was still partial to gender. But now, I sense a bit of a change in her. In today's conversation, she spoke about how her sisters argued against her for "the need to vote." I told her that it does not matter and added:

"What you're standing on is the same platform of crap, shit. Whatever politician is selected will still be standing on this platform of crap. The whole thing must go—Congress included."

"They say that if we don't vote, then the few who vote, say 5% will have—"

"It does not matter," I said emphatically, "Let me tell you a story. Some years ago, the government of Togo in West Africa imposed a housing tax on the population: taxes just like the United States and other developing countries. The people refused in unison. The government officials even used guns to intimidate the house owners. Still, the population refused. No taxes have been paid—no violence required! None! Imagine what would happen if the vast majority of us refuse to join the military. There would be no military. None is needed. I have no confidence in our system."

At this point, I really wanted to tell her that by voting, the voter is actually allowing and participating in evil; and that teachers should not complain about students' misbehavior when it is the teachers who support the leaders and politicians who are directly responsible for the misbehavior. However, I stopped short so that I could tie in the education piece.

"It is no accident that our education does not work. These are the same people bringing the chaos in our education system."

Dawn, November 3, 2011:

When I wake up in the middle of the night and cannot fall back asleep, I just lie in bed idly. This time, however, I decided to focus on the law of attraction.

I tried to go to Mexico in late September of 2011 to eat some Peyote fruit, but the weather prevented me. I was going to use this opportunity to ask for help to get there. I laid in bed with my left temple on the pillow and began calling for help.

"Don Mescalito, help me seek the path to you in the name of the Most Light, Most Pure. I have met with some difficulties. This time around help me find you for my healing." I repeated this line for what appeared ten or more minutes without interruption. To my pleasant surprise, I sensed a presence coming forth toward my face from the center of the bed.

"Don Mescalito," I thought.

Immediately, my face was covered in spider webs. This time around, I knew my prayer was being answered. I was amazed at the speed at which my request had been answered, though I did not consciously know what the answer was.

Later when I would awake, I would think: Spirits can be invoked with mere requests of deep, prolonged, repetitive concentration or prayer. I was fascinated and thankful for the opportunity to perceive beyond the limited five senses without any shamanic training. Thitherto, I had thought that I would need some training to be able to perceive such feasts.

Friday, November 4, 2011: Morning at work: I may be a day off here.

Today my colleagues were back to discussing the school wide discipline issue.

It was during the second period. Two of my female colleagues were in the foreign language office. An ESL teacher, who was older than the Spanish teacher was reading the discipline form. The ESL teacher was sitting down, looking at the Spanish teacher. I was sitting to her right, my eyes on my AP French 4 paper, thinking about how to present my lesson, and thus was not totally engrossed in the conversation. Nevertheless, I was listening.

"They agreed on it," she said, referring to the Assistant Principal of Student Management and the principal, Kathy.

"Absolutely. Such stringent rules are not done in isolation."

The ESL teacher was standing, giggling a little.

"I thought you read it," the Spanish teacher said, laughing a little, "So, you have to be a lawyer…article."

One of my male colleagues walked into the room. The older female ESL teacher turned to him:

"Do you have the manual for discipline?"

Silence ensued. He paused to think. He hedged his words and made a phone call to the Dean's office.

"I don't know. You have to go through all these bureaucratic procedures...," the ESL teacher said.

Upon hanging up the office telephone, my male colleague gave them an answer, which they were not satisfied with.

"We all have to do with less like a business."

I do not recall exactly what the older ESL teacher said next, but my interpretation of my male colleague's answer would be sketched in my mind as "You have to find a way to deal with it."

It was later in the afternoon and I was with my student driver Kevin. We had just exited the bank. As we passed ShopRite on our left, we saw a politician passing out leaflets encouraging passersby to vote for him for the November 8th local elections. An older white woman pushing her shopping cart across the street caught my attention.

"It's the young people we have to reach. If they don't vote, then we're in trouble."

I did not hear what the politician said to the woman, but I knew I was not liking what I was hearing. The grey-haired Caucasian man handed a black pretty woman a leaflet asking her to vote.

"Don't vote!" I said emphatically with a bit of a frown.

"We're standing on the same piece of crap. It doesn't matter who is in power. Look at Obama.

Don't vote!" I raised my voice so that the politician could hear me. I looked at him dead in the eyes. He offered me silence. I walked away, thinking about what had just transpired. Perhaps that was not my mind speaking—my soul?

November 8, 2011:

Education "leaders" and administrators often dish out words like "It's all about the kids." Really? Bull-shit! If it were really about the kids, then they would not be pretending that the new changes in education are supposed to be better for the children. The new wave of "change," labeled the "Common Cores," is designed to standardize learning and the curriculum across all fifty states. The federal legislation on education "No Child Left Behind" is no accident. It is an intentional fraud.

The people behind the legislation and beyond do not wish for any school to perform well. They want chaos in the education system so as they can advance their own agenda of eventually imposing a religion so strong that it would make traditional religions such as Catholicism or Christianity a child's play. This is the religion of science. Let us look at a few facts. NCLB is unconstitutional. The United States Constitution says that States are responsible for education, not the federal government. This is a fact. We spent an entire semester discussing this in one of my education courses.

So, how does the federal government violate the United States Constitution and get away with it? It is simple: *Money*. The federal government tells the States that if they want some *money* to finance their state education system, then this is what each state must do. It is brilliant, for the Feds could always say that it is none obligatory.

Presently, I was at the school's cafeteria with a lot of teachers. It was our school-wide staff meeting to discuss developments in our education field. I turned and watched my colleagues to see if I could guess who was for and against this new way of brainwashing and torturing our children.

We were shown a video about *the Common Cores*. Experts in the education field spoke about the problems they found during their research. These people were either deeply brainwashed or they were agents planted to propagate lies. We will return to this topic later.

As bad as the current education system is, it is still much better than the direction the shadow people want to take us. A while back I saw a 20/20 program titled: "Stupid in America" by John Stossel. It was based on the low performing schools in the District of Columbia public schools. A new chancellor of schools, Michelle Rhee, came to clean up the mess. She met with much resistance, but was able to help students increase test scores. She was highly praised, but the teachers' union found a way to get her fired.

Now, I applaud the chancellor and John Stossel of 20/20 for bringing the education issue to the nation's attention, but for the love of God, can't you both see that the children are not really learning anything?

Test scores went up! Great! What about the fact that our children are learning mostly crap—constant memorization of lies. Have you asked yourselves why they are not learning about who they actually are?

I also recalled the video praising charter schools. It was mentioned that tenure was the problem. That is, the lack of tenure would hold teachers responsible for maintaining high expectations for all of their students to learn better. I beg to differ. How is not giving teachers tenure going to solve the fundamental problems that that our students are not learning anything meaningful? While we're on the topic, I have a couple of friends who are working on a charter school in New York. I was briefly on the board until I saw that this too was a play at the highest level of the pyramid to amalgamate the control over to the private sector: the privatization of education to a global corporation. To see evidence of this, please watch the film College Inc.

November 10, 2011:

There were about two weeks remaining before I went to Mexico for my Peyote healing. As in 2005, I have been having dreams about baring myself to the world: the good and the bad—all of it. When people see you as you are, then you no longer have to censure what you say or how you behave. Instead, the only force that modifies your speech and comportment is the luminosity of Infinity.

Presently, it was 9:33 p.m., and naked dreams of all sorts where I was butt-naked in crowds of people appeared in my mind. I have often wondered about

Freud's theories of the dream state. They did not make sense. But yet, I did not have any other anchor or starting point and so I thought. Once I found myself on top of the sixth floor at the School of International Studies and Public Affairs where Superman, Christopher Reed gave one of his last speeches before departing this world. I was among strangers, naked, but yet could not care at all.

It is only now that I am about to understand the signification of such stark nakedness. I was searching for freedom without borders or superficiality; without embellishments of speech or comportment—to show myself without hiding, without editing. It is only now that I understand: freedom to express myself without being concerned about what others will think. In hindsight, I was searching for the freedom to be myself. Now, I was being more successful at *stopping* the world and myself.

Friday, November 11, 2011:

Today, my mind was bombarding itself with: "How will the future play out? How will you stop those who may come after you?"

"Shush! Do you not remember? Once you were told to stop eating meat to feel better, but you did not: you were shown one world crushing you and for you to escape your stepfather's tyranny. You did not. Once you were told to stay away from the last girl, you did not. Do you not remember how this latter experience hurt? Throughout the years, you have not listened,

Mind. And now you bring up trivial questions about the future?"

The mind was quiet.

"Well, this is the time that you answer without further trivial questioning. Come along for the ride."

And with that I was ready to embark on the next level of stopping my mind and the world.

Three days later, I found myself nearly telling my mind to shut up. The future was now uncertain, thus rendering it more exciting.

A few days have passed and my mind returned to the bull-shit school system. I could not stop thinking about all the bull-shit I was taught in my linguistic courses. One of the most famous linguists and professors of the century is Noel Chomsky. I kept thinking about his bullshit linguistics false propaganda and theories. I was blown back to learn that he is literally part of the control system. I once heard him speak on the Alex Jones internet show. He did not answer a single question honestly, yet this left-brain prisoner talks about how the puppet masters control the system. We have created a *freaken* God out of him when he is spiritually blind. Look at the side he has chosen. So many hours spent memorizing and thinking about his lies—creating a false religion inside my mind—enslaving myself.

Today is Saturday. My trip to Mexico is now very close. I decided to make at least one drug video before heading there. Thus, I assembled my crew and we drove down to New York City to film the video.

Once we arrived in New York City, it took about forty minutes to find my friend Jessica's residence. I was let into the apartment complex by someone with a key. I waited inside the front entrance for about eight or so minutes. During this time, several people entered and exited the building. A group of churchgoers stopped by the door now. There were about four of them. One of them, a young black man stopped to offer me a religious text, to which I said:

"It's ok."

"What we do is to show people that the very design of the human body indicates an intelligent design..."

I did not say anything.

"You don't believe?"

"I don't do religion. It has gotten me in trouble in the past. I don't have any belief systems. Not even science. With that said, we are supposed to know, not believe."

"You don't believe—" he attempted again, "There's definitely life after death."

"What's your name?"

"Agbe."

"Where is it from?"

"I don't indulge in such ephemeral human divisions."

He thanked me politely and left.

Soon after, Jessica came down and we headed to my brother's place to make the Ayahuasca video. The recording lasted for about an hour. I found myself speaking freely without self-censorship. Jessica was definitely taken aback when I said that we are all Gods.

After the video, I made sandwiches for the crew—organic vegan protein slices, and Muenster cheese on soft wheat bread, etc.

After lunch, Jessica and I were talking on the couch. The more we spoke about relationships and life, the closer I fell to her. Yet, I found myself reticent. I experienced a strange feeling inside to hold back. I knew that these were the demons acting up. If you ever watch the video on my website or YouTube, let me say that this was the reason why I was drinking red wine.

As I drove Jessica back home, the same fearful, timid feeling overtook me when she turned to kiss me goodbye on the cheek.

CHAPTER 11

DON PEYOTE SPIRITUAL HEALING

Two or three days before my departure for Real de Catorce, I had an anxiety-filled dream. I immediately recognized it—it was not a new dream. It was either the second or the third time that I had had this nightmarish disturbance. The first time I had it, I really did not understand it. I recalled being in an enclosed area surrounded by shadows—living spirits whose dark vibration I felt as I tried to fly away. Every time I tried to escape, I was brought down with an all-encompassing, suffocating energy. Despite this suffocating feeling, I kept rising until I stood somewhat above the darkness—where I could breathe a little. I awoke with the feeling which translates as:

"You should not go."

This was absurd, for it was full of fear. Besides, I did not know "where" this place that I *shouldn't* go was. As I pondered this negative feeling, it was the same as the time I refused to go to Togo because "the plane might crash." I told myself that if this negative feeling ever transpired again, I would do the exact opposite. The second time I had the dream, it was in the same dark enclosure. This time, the fear was more intense. However, I flew to a nearby populated place where children were playing. There were a few adults nearby. I went into a nearby store, more like a bodega. I came out and flew around, exploring the town a little, mostly walking. This latter aspect was much more enjoyable.

Tuesday, November 22, 2011: 3:10 a.m.:

I rose in my bed. I woke up without the aid of the alarm clock. I was keenly aware that I had no recollection of any dreams that I had that night. I went to the restroom and sat down in the semi-dark room, my head held down, I tried to remember my dreams as I had gotten accustomed to doing every morning. I slept nearly five hours straight without waking up even once. I found it quite curious how I had forgotten the moment I woke up that I was going on a very important journey. It was like forgetting that I had to go to work the next day, which I never do. I felt discomfort within my chest and slightly with my head. A sort of anxiety. A tinge of movement etched in the left side of my head, temple. I had no doubt in my mind that demons remain in my body. As soon as I realized this, I quickly stopped identifying with them.

On the way to the airport, questions of days of old rushed to my mind. One such inquiry was:

"Is this the only planet that is being taken over and being dragged down to a hellish level?"

"Very unlikely," another part of me answered. I raised my head.

"How far does the rabbit hole go?" My mind went to one of the main characters in Dr. Brian Weiss's book Same Soul, Many Bodies.

"Sixty-thousand years ago," Patrick said, "We must stay on Earth with them because our planet is dying and this one is new…True, we needn't have physically come here. Our souls could have been reincarnated into the humans around us or into the beings from other worlds…"

They are really among us now, and some are terrible beings manipulating our world. 60,000 years, hum. And that was not the beginning, for Patrick also said:

"I was born on another planet…When we arrive, others greet us, descendants of beings from earlier migrations from different star systems. They're mixed among an evolving subspecies, human beings."

Somewhere in the recess of my mind, I had already understood that the rabbit hole went deep. However, I was not quite yet ready to accept it until I had further evidence.

November 22, 2011, early afternoon:

I arrived in Mexico City safely. I took the train from the airport to the bus station. I crossed the street and entered the station. I then inquired about my departure to Matehuala. The place was bustling with people. I searched around for a seat. I found one near a flat screen television to my left in the back.

"May I sit down?" I asked the young lady sitting on the other side.

"Of course."

"Thank you."

I turned to look at the television. There was a program about serving one's country by joining the army. A few young men were shown firmly holding weapons with both hands with pride. I faced forward in my seat. I was facing the girl now.

"I don't understand how by killing and thus destroying your soul, you're protecting your country."

"The government requires it," she said.

I turned around about ninety degrees to watch a bit more. When I had enough, I turned to face her again.

"Where are you from?" she asked.

"God," I answered, indulging with a smile.

She paused to consider my statement with a pondering countenance.

"What's your name?"

"Agbe. It means life. What's your name?"

"Emma."

"Ah! The writer," I said, searching for the famous English author's name.

"Jane Austen," she said.

"Where are you going?"

"Real de Catorce."

"Have you been there before?"

"When I was three years old."

"So you know what Peyote is?"

"Yes," she answered, looking at my Ayahuasca bracelet.

"Do you speak English?"

"Some."

"I got this in Peru," I said, raising my left hand so that Emma could have a full view.

Reader, let me put the facts on the table now so that I may be better understood later. Yes, I did think Emma was pretty. However, at no time during our conversation did I consider "hitting on her." Recall that my last long relationship did not work.

From Mexico City to Real de Catorce:

At 9:52 p.m. I handed my suitcase to the man standing by the luggage area of the bus. The suitcase handler looked at my ticket.

"Real de Catorce," I said to him.

"Ah, Peyote!" he said, smiling, indicating that he knew why I was going."

"It's for spiritual cleansing," I said, "to get rid of negative 'energies' in my body."

He was surprised.

"Most people don't take if for that."

"It's like Ayahuasca. Do you know Ayahuasca?"

Most people don't, but he did. I went to the front of the bus where a lady was handing out sandwiches and bottles of water as we boarded. I took only the water, for I was not sure if the food was really natural; and besides, I saw meat in the sandwiches. With the exception of the gangster-style film playing loudly, the bus ride was quite comfortable. The seat actually had a foot rest to support my calves.

Matehuala:

This is a city that is about an hour and half from Real de Catorce. I arrived there at about 5:30 a.m. I bought a bus ticket at the counter for 7:45 a.m. At 7:30 I tried to exit the door that would lead me to the bus area, but was stopped by a lady sitting by the door. She asked me for the "unidad." I had no idea what she was talking about. As a result, she wasted my time and caused me to miss the bus. The lady at the counter complained about the woman at the door having done this before. I asked her if there were any immediate solutions for me because talking about her was not going to help me resolve my problem. She told me that I had no choice but to wait for another three and a half hours. I went into a small restaurant at the bus station and began working on this very book you are reading now.

Several hours later, I was finally on the bus. The driver made a few stops as we neared the town. The houses were constructed entirely out of rocks, stones, and some bricks. I did not see any vegetation. *I wondered how the people here survive without crops.* Finally, we reached our final destination which left me perplexed. I asked the conductor what I was supposed to do. He told me to get into another bus, which was to my left. This bus was more rustic: older. I had to carry my suitcase inside and there was nowhere to place it. I went to the back, still no place to put my belongings. Finally, I placed the suitcase in between the aisle, which fit tightly. I managed to turn my body around, while nearly smacking an old woman to my left.

"I am sorry," I said to her, "I just wanted to see where we are going."

The lady next to her asked me where I was from. I was going to give her my standard answer, but there was something about her countenance that compelled me to give her a basic answer.

"Where are *you* from?"

"Puerto Rico," she said, "You see I'm much farther than you."

"What brings you here? Family?"

"I'm here to bury my brother."

I offered her silence for two or three seconds then told her that I was sorry for her lost.

We came to a tunnel, which I would learn later was called "El Tunel Orgarrio."

The driver came to a full stop. I wondered what he was waiting for to enter, for I saw no traffic signals. The thought occurred to me that he was waiting for it to be safe before he went in, but "how could he tell?" I saw no indication for this. Finally, he entered the tunnel. As soon as he entered, it was like a light dawning in my head.

"Oh! The tunnel!" The thought occurred to me that this was the place the dark entities were trying to suffocate me. I understood immediately that these demons were once again trying to stop me from seeking spiritual healing.

When we arrived at our final destination, the baggage person pointed to a boy who would take me to my hotel. He was about ten years old. A man approached, trying to take me on a tour to some sort of church for 180 pesos. I told him that I was there for spiritual cleansing. I turned to the boy who immediately pointed to a guy. Señor Carlos came to introduce himself, and we spoke briefly.

"How much is it?"

"350 pesos," he answered, "Is it ok?"

"Yes," I said.

Don Carlos looked at his watch. The boy told him where my hotel was.

"I'll come get you at 2:30 p.m."

"Why don't we make it 3 p.m.?" I said, thinking I needed a little more time to get settled into the hotel.

"We have four hours to travel by horse: round trip."

"Alright, I'll see you at 2:30 p.m. in front of the hotel."

The boy and I went into "an alley" whose ground were made out of pure rocks—light grey. I handed him a 50-peso bill and walked the rest of the way to the hotel. About twenty minutes later, don Carlos came for me. We went to an "alleyway." There, a young man was attending to a black-like mull. On the other side of the street was a white horse.

"Let him ride this one," he said to his son.

Then don Carlos showed me how to turn the horse left, right, as well as how to stop him. I told him that I had only ridden a horse once and it was not for long. We were off. His dog accompanied us. It did not take me long before I got the jest of steering Paloma, my horse. He kept getting too close to the left where the steep cliff descended.

About forty-five minutes later, I had a déjà-vu. I looked around. The area was exactly as in the vision that I had when Mother Earth let me explore the planet in Light form.

"I've already been here," I said to don Carlos.

"Yeah?" he inquired.

"Yes, in a vision...*Interesting,*" I said, as if talking to myself.

Another half an hour passed. My guide told me how a lot of people lost their lives by accidently driving off the cliff. I learned that the number 14 in the town's name is significant. According to don Carlos, there was an incident where 14 people die. Furthermore, *real* was also once used as a monetary exchange in the town.

About fifty minutes later, we came to a little store to our left. Don Carlos said we had to purchase some soft drinks to offset the bitter taste of Peyote. We bought two bottles of orange beverages. About half an hour near our final destination, he began talking again.

"Peyote is very difficult to find."

“Isn’t it green like those over there?” I inquired, pointing to the left side of the desert.

“No, they are like the rocks. They are hard to find. An ordinary tourist could search for hours without a guide.”

“I am told that I should not eat the first Peyote that I see, and that I am supposed to talk to him first.”

“That’s right,” he concurred, “Did you learn about Peyote through the internet?”

“Yes.”

A while later, don Carlos told me to turn left, and that we were going to camp there. He secured the horses, then helped me find some Peyote. I *talked* to the first one that I saw with my mind. I thanked him in advance for the healing I was about to receive. I also thanked don Mescalito for visiting me before my arrival there. Then, don Carlos showed me how to pick the Peyote. We picked about six. I washed and put them to my left on a grey piece of rock. When I was ready to consume them, don Carlos brought me the orange soft drink and some water. I then took out my phone and asked him to record me eating them. I chewed as he recorded my medicinal enterprise. After recording me for a while, he turned around to capture the surrounding ambiance.

“This isn’t so bad,” I said in Spanish. However, after I finished chewing my second fruit, I could not wait to finish off with the whole affair. It was really bitter. After the fourth, I washed my mouth with the orange beverage, and waited a few seconds before engaging the last two. Finally, I was done.

“I finished,” I said with a triumphant smile.

“Bueno,” my guide answered.

I took out my sturdy little pillow that I brought from New York. I lied down and put my head on it. A minute later, I turned to don Carlos.

"What's the plan?"

"We'll stay here for a while."

I looked at my phone. It was 5:30 p.m.

"It'll take about forty-five minutes for the effect to kick in. I don't want to get caught up here in the dark. We should go. I can always vomit on the way."

And so, I was on my white stallion once again.

The ride back was not at all comfortable. Every time Paloma started picking up speed, my stomach became unsettled. I knew the medicine was at work. About forty minutes later, I reached into my left pocket and took out my phone to look at the time. We came upon lights at the distance to our right.

"Do you see that?" I exclaimed, "Do you see the lamps' rays?"

"No," he said.

"Is it just me? You don't see the lights' bright rays? They are at least five feet wide—circular."

"It must be the Peyote." I closed my eyes for a brief second and a half to determine if I would see something. I saw a circular object in the form of Peyote radiating its colors in four segments—black, green, and I think yellow. I opened my eyes, lest I fell off the cliff. My stomach became more upset.

"Look at the stars," my guide said. I turned to my left.

"That one there is a satellite. That one is a star."

"No, it's not!" I exclaimed, "Can't you see its rays? The way it shines. It's shining just like the lamps. The rays are long—as if fabricated. It's a satellite," I said.

He wanted to continue talking, but I could not.

"I don't feel like talking now. I feel nauseous," I said, but realized that he did not understand. I had used the wrong words in Spanish. I explained myself briefly and stopped talking. It seemed I had been on the desert mountain for days. I was having difficulty guiding the horse, who every once in a while seemed to veer too far to the right toward the cliff. At other times, it seemed that Paloma was guiding me. I wanted to close my eyes, but I knew I could not. At one point, I could have sworn that I saw dark spirits flying by. I ignored them, thinking that it was the effect of the Peyote. However, when this kept reoccurring, I had to reconsider my assumption. Paloma came to a stop twice to catch his breath.

"He's tired," I said to don Carlos.

"Just a little."

When we were about fifteen minutes away from home, some vicious dogs came out of nowhere. They ran at our horses. Our day companion fought them off. Finally, we arrived. Don Carlos's son came to greet us. Paloma went directly to his drinking quarters. He knew he was home.

"I'm going to walk him to the hotel."

As we began walking, I was seized by the throat. I threw my yellow bag over my left shoulder and vomited like there was no tomorrow. *So, this is what you were afraid of? This is what you tried to cause me to fear?"*

Negative souls floated above my head, making fearful noise. It was like being back in the Ayahuasca ceremony, but this time a little different. What I coughed out was dark, solid mass-like structure. I knew immediately why: The darkest of the darkest souls were the last to go. Up ahead was a young man slightly shouting with joy:

"It's the medicine!"

"Yes," I somehow managed to say. I barely recognized him. Don Carlos advised me to sit down a little. I did. About a minute later, I was back on my feet.

"We must get back to the hotel."

As soon as I had said that I was vomiting again.

"Let's go," he said, looking a little worried. He walked me for less than a minute before pointing ahead, saying where the hotel was. I did not understand, but it was too late. He was gone! I stopped walking to orient myself. To my left was El Bar Molino. *I remember this, but where's the hotel?* I was confused, but I kept walking toward two women who were conversing about something in Spanish. I was in the middle of the intersection now. A dark spirit flew by my left. I looked up, and finally I was relieved. I was able to make out the word "Alamos." I went inside and climbed three floors to get to my hotel room 30. Upon entering the room, I threw my yellow bag down next to the right side where the chair and desk were. I briefly considered not showering before going to bed. I quickly searched for the bar of soap in my suitcase. I was not finding my African sponge fast enough, so I abandoned the task and went into the bathroom. There were two metallic knobs. I turned on the first one without thinking. There was a bright yellow C marked on it. One might have thought that I would have figured this out quickly given that I speak Spanish, right? Naw! My mind was elsewhere. I was too fascinated by the living colors. I looked at the shower knob. The little green openings were moving outward. The green was dazzling. I turned around to receive the warm water on my back. I seized the soap. Its *brown* was also transforming right before my very eyes. It was as if the *brown* was separating into yellow—the yellow as coming out of the brown; as if the soap was not really brown to begin with. I turned to my left. The yellow "C" written on the first shower knob extended itself thin into the air toward me. I heard the water drip on my body as I struggled to regain my former three-dimensional consciousness. This was not at all what I was expecting. I was happy enough that I had vomited out the demons.

As much as I resisted being in this altered state, I could not help but sneak a little look at the wall from where the water was flowing. The grey and marble titles started closing in on me. They were literally moving!

"Wow!"

"What is your objective Agbessi?" I found myself saying out loud.

"To take a shower," I answered inside my head.

Somehow, I managed to finish taking the shower. I got out and went to the night table to pick something up. For the life of me, I could not recall what piece of metal I picked up, but it began to disintegrate into the atmosphere right in front of me. To me, it was losing its individual identity—becoming an unidentified part of the air. I looked at my left hand, and as I focused on it, it started doing the same thing as the piece of metal. I was losing the capacity to distinguish my hand from everything else.

"No way!"

I quickly put my hand away from my eyes' view, lest I should lose it permanently into the air and everything else around me. *I can still maintain my individual identity even as I fade into the Whole? Fantastic!* I liked it. *So, this is what it means to become nothing.*

I turned toward my bed and picked up my Ayahuasca bracelet. I wanted to place it nearer the pillow so that it would not fall from the bed. Before I knew it, the green and the orange colors launched themselves at me in waves of fluid energy. They moved toward me in the air.

"Far out!" I felt like I was going to lose control of my reality if I did not stop looking at things. I quickly placed my necklace next to my Ayahuasca bracelet. Though my eyes only caught the bracelet for a moment, the brown started turning to deep red while still maintaining an element of the brown. *Exotic!* Even this color seemed to have a will of its own.

"Even colors are alive?" I asked.

"Yes!" I can think straight.

My soul was right above me. I was aware of his presence and it was immediately clear who He was. For the life of me, I could not recall the exact words he said. There were several things transpiring concomitantly—the voices of the neighbors outside, which I was distinctively aware of, female voices, and something about the "pipes." I heard a gurgling noise as well. My soul said something. I do not recall the exact words. Only the intuitive understanding remained with me. I was in bed with my eyes open. My soul said something else.

"I need no permission to exist," I answered aloud with a determined but calm force. At that moment I was aware of the fact that I was speaking loudly enough for the neighbors to hear me, but I did not seem to care. My soul seemed to be in the center of my body.

"Remember why you give thanks to the food you eat…"

I immediately understood this futuristic message as a warning about the possible imbalance in confidence in my mind. In other words, there is a difference between confidence and "crossing the line." For me crossing the line was being tough, blatant, bordering insult when I see how stubbornly selfish humanity is being.

"Human beings do not yet have the technical know-how to create the tools necessary to harness energies such as the sun to allow them not to eat living things such as animals and plants."

I knew I was crying happy tears, but my eyes were nearly dry. This was an answer to the question for which I have waited a long time: the vegetable and fruit dilemma.

I thought that the fruit and vegetable revelation was exhilarating, but what transpired next blew my mind into pieces across the Universe, metaphorically speaking.

My soul took a physical form—that of my current physical self. He manifested a folder.

"You've been on both sides," he said firmly.

"Annunaki?" I wondered, but he did not answer. He repeated his statement as if to say that it does not matter if I were on the side of good or bad. I understood immediately that he was talking about the "highly evolved" alien civilizations. This was my rabbit hole question.

"When you speak now you'll be heard across the frequencies."

I understood this as going beyond this planet—across other dimensions.

This was mind boggling.

"No deception will come from *them*. You will speak 100% truth," he said. He was talking about a "highly evolved" ET council who tried to kill me in 2009.

What happened next confirmed for me that great deception exists across our Universe and knows no race or extraterrestrial limit. I was being shown how the information would be passed when an extraterrestrial being in light form sneaked past us. Then my soul took me to "the past." It was life times that I had experienced beyond this Earthly dimension. Reader, I saw people just like you and I, but not. My mind went *"wow!"* for I was dumbfounded. I had just travelled to a past incarnation, but not. It was not the past. Furthermore, I surmised that it was at least 10,000 years in the future. I have always said that time does not exist, but somehow I fell under the illusion that reincarnation occurred in a chronological, logical time order. And there I was being proven wrong.

"You still don't believe?" my soul said with a determined frown. "Ok, let's do it again!"

He brought me back to my room and started again. This time, I was hearing him say the most astounding thing:

"Superman has been created, but has no spirituality."

"How can this be more than 10,000 years in the future? I've been reincarnated into the past?"

Then, in thought form he said:

"The supermen who were created are destroying the world."

By this, I knew he meant the future. Back in my room, I looked at the white curtain and the brown wooden frame in bewilderment.

"You don't believe in time travel?" the masculine voice boomed out, as if he were tired of my stubbornness.

After the sixth or seventh time, my soul said again:

"Ok, not enough? Let's do it again!"

The right side of my brain was hurting now. It was as if it were being rewired to accept the new truths. We went through that future life time and time again. My soul's words "Superman has already been created, but has no spirituality" hit me crystal clear now—and my mind again uttered "wow!"

"The current education system! There is no spirituality in it—no matter where you go in the world. It's coordinated to blind us, to worship the intellect—to be brilliant beyond imagination and to have powers, but not to know who we really are. This is one of the major ways they're creating the supermen of the future."

I felt and saw what he was showing me briefly, but could not recall the details of what he was saying. The feeling that I would take with me, however, would be immense. Later, when I would have had the chance to absorb the information, I would understand how one could be programmed to have superhuman powers and not be aware of one's ultimate Light Self. The left brain works in compartments. It is like having separate boxes—each box working only one at a time. Whole or several boxes are not opened at the same time to make the connection between the individual pieces. This is where the right brain or the spiritual self comes in. The right brain is able to open several boxes at the same time and to make links between them. For instance, our young people are currently being taught that different species such as mammals and animals cannot mate and conceive hybrid species. How ludicrous this is if you've ever seen a mermaid or a human being with tails like an ape in Africa. How ludicrous it is if one actually knows what is happening with "transhumanism" and the combination of human and animal genes to form new human hybrids. Hasn't science maintained that such a feast was not possible because animals and humans are different species? Yes, it has purposely claimed so in order to confuse people. This is the kind of lies witchcraft and Satanist practitioners such as Charles Darwin have sought to confuse us about what is possible in the Universe.

After these feelings sunk in my mind firmly, I could no longer deny the fact that something terrible went wrong in the future that went beyond this third dimension and is affecting a lot of other dimensions in the universe.

By the time my soul took me through this cycle the eighth or the ninth time, it had been engrained in me that I had been brought back to the "past" to help rectify this future problem. When my soul was convinced that I had no more doubt, He took me to another scene, where a few people were reaching out their hands to me. This was symbolic of them offering their assistance in my spiritual development.

Then came the severe scolding.

"Next time you're worried about what people will think about you, remember the bigger picture."

This was said in a firm voice and left an almost indelible image in my mind. More images of people suffering flooded the scene. I reached out my hand to help those suffering take mine. As I did this, I began to cry.

"There's too much at stake."

I knew my Light Self was partially talking about the "education" video that I was hesitating to make because of the way my fellow teachers may view me.

I turned over to my left in my sleep, but sleep would not come. I lied in bed for what appeared to be about 30-40 minutes. I was not sure, but it could not have been more than forty-five minutes later when my telephone alarm clock began ringing. It was six o'clock in the morning. I clearly recall looking at the clock when I entered my room. It was only a few minutes past 8 p.m. (8:07 I believe). That meant that I had been time traveling for about nine hours.

I turned my alarm clock off and attempted to sleep for two hours before getting out of bed.

I went to the bathroom to shower.

"Shouldn't someone else be doing this?" I said aloud as I turned on the shower water. I mean, ever since I was a child I have always wanted to do something important, but this was way too much for my mind. I had no idea what I would be taking on. I was no longer happy. The rabbit

Black Magic was no longer working on me. My intent to maintain a straight path is unbending.

I turned my mind to my Ayahuasca experience. Recall that I was aware that the ground could *feel* just like me.

Later, when I had had the chance to digest the experience, I would understand that my vegetable question had been mainly answered: vegetables and fruits have the capacity to feel like us; but there are levels of awareness, and that animals and fish feel more intense physical sensation when they are killed for human consumption.

When I would return to the States, I would type in the word "vegan" into Google. The definition would read: Veganism is a type of vegetarian diet that excludes meat, eggs, dairy products and all other animal-derived ingredients. I understood this to mean that vegans do not eat fish, cheese or drink milk. Then I thought:

"What would the vegan say about the ground being alive?"

If one were foolish enough to seize a bunch of soil from the ground and to put it into one's mouth and to somehow manage to digest it with a bit of water, the soil that has been consumed would still be alive.

As I sat at my desk in the afternoon, the full wave of comprehension of my soul's warning dawned on me. I understood beyond measure that the message was absolutely accurate. I understood that I was no longer going to tolerate such false abusive belief systems aimed at keeping me a prisoner. Somehow my soul had seen a point in the near future where the mind surpassed a high confidence level and teetered on "toughness" or "meanness." I did not want to be mean to people, but I no longer wanted to hear them speak about the global slave system as if it were a great thing. The thing with such experiences is that they happened with people across the world, no race was an acceptation.

One such conversation came to me crystal clear. I was back at Columbia University at the University Residence Hall. I was behind the Help Desk with a colleague. He too was African, but Black Muslim. On the other side of the counter were two other black students. One of them was from somewhere in East Africa. We were in the middle of a conversation.

"But how could you be proud of your culture? I don't understand. Isn't one 'proud' of something one has done? An accomplishment? Whether we are Black or White, we are born into our cultures—something inherited."

"I will always be proud to be African!" she beamed at me with a scornful frown.

My tall male co-worker laughed slightly, more or less saying the same thing as the agitated East African girl. It was clear that they were mocking me. I felt my inner voice receding, and I offered them silence. My Ghanaian "countryman" was making no effort to understand that I was trying to speak beyond the physical—from an intuitive level. Even then when I was deeply confused about who I was beyond the physical, I knew that they were in a worse place then I was. Their *minds* were deeply imbedded in the superficial world. They were defending one of the absurd, false belief systems—culture; and there I was trying to have a truth seeking conversation with them calmly; and they were shutting me down—shutting me down because of their mostly false cultural belief system, whose falseness they wanted everybody else to accept out of pure blindness.

The above example was just one discussion of many that I had over the years. Most people were like prisoners trying to make sure the other *more* awakened prisoners do not escape from prison. They did this with the imposition of their false belief systems. And so, I immediately understood the message my soul was trying to convey to me. The message was understood as "don't go overboard when you refuse to listen to nonsense of days of old." The truth is that I had been using the law of attraction "to stop" the nonsense of not only my mind, but also that of the world.

Furthermore, after I would return to the United States from the Peyote experience, the extent to which I would care about the nonsense people spew about God and the nature of existence would have very little effect on me. Once they called me "crazy" and "weird;" now I looked at them as the insane ones. The extent to which people were asleep in an amnesiatic state was no longer surprising to me. Within a few days, I started taking my soul's warning seriously. I even went back to read notes that I had taken from one of Carlos Castaneda's books: "Peyote teaches you how to live." I had learned how to live—how to stop my mind from following an impassive road.

The only thing that I did not understand immediately was the message about the girl. I still questioned the fact that I was not aware that Emma was placed in front of me on purpose. I mean, I believed him, but I would say to my soul that He was not firm enough with me. Even as I wrote the previous sentence, I wondered if I were in some shape or form unconsciously trying to evade responsibilities for my past decisions.

Sunday, November 25, 2011:

I arrived at the Chicago airport to transfer planes. I waited in a long customs line. Eventually, I was called to the side of an empty line. I thought I would be going through the usual security scan. For the first time, I was asked by one of the security personnel to submit myself to a full body radiation scanner.

"These things have radiation," I said in protest.

"It's just a small dose," the young White woman said without the slightest inkling of critical thinking. She looked about 30 years old.

"Yeah, it's not happening. I'll take the physical pat down."

"Where should I wait for you?"

"I can't check you."

"Why not?" I asked, fully knowing the answer.

"To avoid possible lawsuit."

"You're going to have a guy do it?"

"Sit over there," she said pointing to her left, to the regular security check. To my left was a tall full-body young white girl.

"It'll just take a moment…" she said with a slight frown.

"That's alright. I've heard these arguments before."

"You might miss your flight."

"Oh, I have plenty of time."

It was obvious that she was a blind follower of the system who lives in cognitive dissonance. She knew very well that these full-body scanners have radiation, yet her brain ignored it.

sense to me because during the Peyote experience, my soul said that dark souls hide in negativity. To me, this was a delightful reinforcement of the warning that my soul had given me.

I also became aware of a very important general truth: It does not cost you anything to let go and to help even those who have caused you harm. In fact, when you do this, you are automatically helping Infinity (i.e., God). When one rises, the Whole rises.

Tuesday, January 24, 2012:

I was proctoring the midterm and the Regents exams. Ever since my Peyote experience, I had been thinking about spiritual progress in general. That is, how slow and fast souls can elevate their Light and my last experience about reincarnation and time travelling. I was still not convinced about the time travelling aspect of my visions. Are the past and the future converging?

Who has the files? 10,000 years of information?

I could not be sure who was actually on both sides. *My future self?* I could not be sure that it was indeed me the Mind who has had these experiences. I thought that it was possible that it had been my soul. However, never in all my years has my Light Self lied to me. He never, ever lies.

"You've been on both sides," my soul said.

Yeah, he definitely used the pronoun "you" to describe my experiences. Yeap, he was keeping it simple for me. *It is my future self that had the experiences. Perhaps these are details to him? Perhaps I am in denial?*

So, time really does not exist in a chronological order. What could be has already happened. Is this a different timeline? A parallel universe I am living in because these are the dominant thoughts I wish to explore?

I was not sure how one could have two separate beings of the same soul existing at the same. Are there bits and pieces of the same soul in different dimensions and parallel universes? How? I did not understand and definitely needed more information.

"When the observer becomes the observed, the very thing being observed must change."

Hasn't the game changed a long time ago once the negative entities attacked me in bed? Or was this part of my life plan?

I have a feeling my mind is going to be blown again in Costa Rica in April 2012.

Tuesday, January 26, 2012:

"But I don't remember...*who* has been on both sides?"

You see Reader, I may have my problems, but I have prided myself on doing the right thing. So, thousands of years from now but not. *How could I have been on both sides?*

To be on the side of the none positive implies negativity. And if I would in the future be on the side of the negative, then what would compel me to do this. Or, perchance this life time is a parallel universe giving me the chance to rectify what has already been done. This latter possibility seems to make more sense, for I know that this current Agbessi would never join the dark side. Pain or suffering is a powerful reminder to do the right thing. Even as I write now, I have at least one negatively powerful demon in my neck and shoulders. Every few minutes I have had to crack my neck and shoulders to feel a little better. One thing is for sure: beings in this universe are very sneaky. Still, I wonder. If anything, this experience of learning what has already occurred in the future will help me completely *stop* my mind, and I guess make me more neutral and not to separate myself like an island.

February 2012:

Overall, I feel that I have been successful at not indulging in short-lived pleasures such as sex and eating meat. In terms of sex, it has been nearly a year since I have had any. Apropos meat, I have not had any since 2009. I have not had any difficulty maintaining my diet. However, I cannot say the same for the remaining negative entity or entities in my body.

I have had manipulative "dreams" which attempted to convince me that it was alright to consume meat. The last food dream occurred after I returned from Mexico in November of 2011. In the dream, I found myself in an office full of cubicles. There were people (mostly women) eating, laughing, and having a great time. This, I would take as an unconscious message for me to resume eating meat. *Fat chance!* All I had to think about was how my friend the ram was slaughtered that day. He lied on the ground like a piece of "nothing."

I also had manipulative dreams about sex. In one of these dreams, I saw two men making "love." It was so raw and physical that I thought they were going to bit each other's face off. I brushed it off as a bad dream.

After my first Peyote session, it became clearer that the urges were not coming from me: they were coming from the demons trying to get their fix.

Throughout these experiences, only one thing really abated the sexual desires—red wine. I believe it was in late October when I gave up none organic red wine and started drinking only organic wine. There were two problems with this. First, it was costing me a lot of money. Second, the more I drank each night, the more I needed to drink to get the desired drowsy effect to fall asleep.

Thursday, February 16, 2012:

I arrived at the Mexican capital at about 2:15 p.m. The plane was late. Upon retrieving my luggage, I sat down, opened my suitcase and began eating a small bag of organic toasted corn nuts with some sparkling water that I brought from New York. Then, I called to reserve a room at the Hotel Alamos, where I last stayed at Real de Catorce. After that, I went to purchase a bus ticket for Matehuala. The same lady who sold me the last bus ticket about three months thither reminded me that I needed to take the train to "El Norte" bus station.

On my way there I thought about possibly meeting Emma. I arrived there at about 5 p.m. Since I met her there at nearly three months ago at about 7:30 p.m. I was hoping, just hoping that she might be there again—out of pure

"I'll go to the desert and bring the fruit to you. What do you think?"

"Alright, sounds like a good idea," I said.

He looked at his watch.

"It's about ten o'clock now, I'll be back at 1 or 2 o'clock."

"I'll come down, but if you don't see me, then look for me in room 25 of Alamos, the hotel."

He handed me the rope to direct his donkey and he rode Paloma to the desert. About five minutes later, I met his son on the road. He took the donkey and began riding him while I walked. I was dying of hunger when I returned to Real. I thought about eating, but knew it would mess up my first Peyote session. Thus, I decided to do a few errands to occupy my time and mind. On my way to the Leonardo's place, I saw a woman with a young lady selling some decorative souvenirs at the intersection of Calle Lendo and Calle Zaragoza. She showed me a "blue" stone bracelet.

"It's for a student…People want everything I'm wearing."

"You have good vibes," she said, smiling.

"Ok, but will it fit?"

She put it on her wrist and it did fit. We spoke a little more: She did most of the talking. She caught my attention when she said that there is no such thing as fear.

"All the bad things you are experiencing come from inside," she said, pointing to her temple.

She was referring to people in general, and I agreed for the most part.

"Yes, there is no fear, but entities, whether they are demons exist independently of us."

As we spoke, it was evident to me that she was convinced that the demons inside us are our own creation. I stopped talking. It was only yesterday when I heard this belief system. Recall that the painter Leonardo said the same thing. I thought about Jonathan, the "psychic" healer in New York advancing the same idea. By the way Reader, I do think that there is some truth to this, but to accept this idea as the only reason for one's depression or negative spiritual experience is utter folly. I decided to leave Maria and her daughter Escandy and to go pay Leonardo the rest of the money for the demon drawings. Just as I was about to leave, I heard a familiar question.

"Where are you from?"

"The Universe," I heard myself say. She was laughing slightly, and her daughter even more intensely.

"Ok, good luck on your journey here on planet Earth."

"You too!" Maria answered as I walked away.

I was at Leonardo's house two or three minutes later. We conversed briefly and I paid him the rest of the money and left.

On my way back, I took a picture of the alleyway and the mountain. I stopped to converse with Maria again.

"How do you deal with the cold at night?" I asked her.

"Where are you staying?"

"The Hotel Alamos."

"Yeah, it's cold there."

I was walking away when she asked to take a picture with me. Her daughter took it with her phone. I asked her daughter to take one for me with my phone as well, which she did. Maria then offered me her coat made out of wool.

"You can borrow it."

I thought about it briefly and accepted. I was soon to learn why she said that the negative spiritual manifestations that one experienced were from oneself.

She was saying the most bizarre thing.

"You should go to the desert to cut the Peyote yourself. A connection is created when you cut it yourself. I had some negative experiences, images when I first took it," she said, implying that someone had cut it for her.

"The person who cuts it creates a connection to the plant, which could be bad."

I believed her, but her comments did not worry me, for I recalled the last dream that I had about a month and a half ago when I felt total liberation from the entities in my body. What caught my attention about what Maria was saying was that I did not mention anything even remotely close to her about don Carlos getting the Peyote for me. I was sure she had guessed or was being intuitive.

Interestingly, less than a week before embarking on my journey to Real, my mother indirectly tried to discourage me from coming by saying that she heard on the mainstream ABC News that a warning had been given to all American travelers not to go to Mexico.

"Dada, it's the mainstream media. What do you expect?"

"They actually used the word 'prohibited.' They're killing Americans in Mexico."

"Please!" I said, brushing off her fear, "Nothing is going to stop me from going."

I returned my mind to the conversation with Maria.

"The last time I came here don Carlos was the one who cut the Peyote for me. Nothing bad happened. I experienced the demons, but that was it. I still have quite a bit inside. They're killing my neck."

"Where is he from?"

"Here," I answered, "Don't worry, it'll be alright."

"I write and share my spiritual experiences with people…"

"I am a 'writer' too," I said.

I learned that she lost her parents at the age of fifteen and felt "vueca," which she explained to me is a feeling of emptiness. She had suffered a lot. Ayahuasca and Peyote helped her. I jokingly told her that Mother Ayahuasca helped me a lot too and that I was in love with her. She laughed at the idea of me being in love with Mother Ayahuasca. Given that she said that she shared her stories with people and the fact that she had lived in Real for 17 years, I decided to pose her questions about the town. Some customers arrived and she turned to them. Her daughter walked up a few feet to where I was and took her place.

"I'm going to put this in my second book. Have you ever taken Peyote?"

"Yes."

"How was it—the experience?"

"I learned about people in Mexico."

That was it. She did not say anything else.

"Everyone's experience is different. How long have you lived here?"

"I have been here for sixteen years."

"Let's talk about the food. People go to other towns to purchase their food?"

"Most of the food comes from there," she said, pointing to the right side of the desert.

"I hear the town used to be bustling with people and mining activities."

"It was much smaller before," she said, pointing directly in front of us.

"Over there, beyond the church," her mother added.

Escandy said that the town was called Fantasmo or something to that effect.

"Why? Were there ghosts there?" I asked smiling.

"No," she answered, laughing.

"Maybe at night," her mother answered.

"I was told that the number 14 is significant to the town's name. Fourteen people died."

"Fourteen Spanish bandits who came to open up the mines. They died," she added.

"They met their deaths here?"

"Yes," she answered.

Interesting! I told myself. No action is ever overlooked.

Saturday, February 18, 2012: Afternoon and Evening:

At 3 p.m. there was a knock on the door. It was don Carlos. He reached into his left shirt pocket, and I went to get a green biodegradable plastic bag for him to put the Peyote fruit in. He took out six.

"They are big. That one there can count as two."

"Six?" I said in wonder; I wanted eighteen. Then, he dug into his other inside pocket and took out six more. Three of them were small.

"Twelve? Well, that's better than nothing. You were afraid that something bad would happen, right?"

"Yes," he said, his facial expression concurring with his answer.

"Don't worry! It's ok," I said with a Puerto Rican accent, "My soul can handle it."

"It doesn't go outside this room," he said a bit worried.

"Of course. I know."

"Come see me at the other end of the tunnel on Monday when you're leaving."

"There won't be enough time."

"Ok then come by the house at 6 p.m. It's right by…"

"I'll remember how to get there," I said.

He had shown me his house on Friday evening when I saw him.

The time was now 4:59 p.m. and the Peyote journey had begun. It took me until 5:52 p.m. to finish eating the fruit. I had much difficulty chewing and swallowing it. The taste was much bitter then I remembered the last time. I took a shower a while ago, spitting out its bitterness.

The time is now 6:24 p.m., and I had just exited the shower and looked at my cell phone. A nauseous feeling began eight minutes ago. I was in front of my laptop, at the wooden desk, listening to Adele "Set Fire to the Rain." I waited for the vomit to come. Thoughts of going to bed and having a good, tranquil sleep crossed my mind.

I closed my eyes and felt pulsating colors.

"What was that dream I had months ago after the first Peyote experience?"

In that dream, I saw myself sitting on some sort of a chair—a throne and before me was a deep cliff, which if I got too close would be the end of me.

I closed my eyes again. The pulsating colors increased on the sides. I put my head down. *Bed?* There is a rumbling chair noise coming from the floor above me. I looked at the clock. It was 6:47 p.m. I cracked my neck with my right hand while maintaining a black pen between my fingers.

"Why is Adele setting fire to the rain? Bed?"

I felt palpitations in my left and right legs. I also felt nausea: only slightly. *Bed?* It is definitely cold in the room.

Must let go of all ego that binds me to a static state of perception.

I began to pray. "Peace to all, even those who will exit. Peace to my slightly rumbling stomach…" A happy thought briefly occupied my mind. Smile *Agbe. When it's over, I'll have a nice sleep. All divergent roads lead to one clear, luminescent road.*

I turned away the chair that was holding my jacket, so not to vomit on it.

The time is now 6:50 p.m. The nauseous feeling has increased to the point that it has been uncomfortable sitting down.

"Wanna go to bed," a part of me said.

"No, you'll vomit on the sheets. Wait!" I heard another part of me say.

After a few minutes, writing became nearly impossible. I focused on Adele's song "...Given up so easily. I thought you loved me more than this."

I smiled and thought about a past ex-girlfriend.

"Turn off music and computer?"

"No, I am enjoying the music. Not yet! The shadow! The shadow must go!"

I turned to the window to observe the mountains. The crease between the lower and the center layers appeared infinitely more distinct...Finally, two house lights came on. They shone forth brightly below the mountain range.

At 7:17 p.m. I stared into the water in the rectangular plastic orange trash can. I saw nothing but an ugly face staring back at me. I smiled to see if the image would change. It did, but it was a bizarre reflection. After a few minutes, I went to put the water bin next to the dark, small table.

About half an hour later, I quickly turned to the water bin to vomit. Nothing came out. I purposely kept coughing in order to get whatever it was that I was feeling out of my throat. I held my chest and throat, and then shook my head up and down, and from right to left. As I did this, I felt a grip around my head. It was a little physical though you could not see it: *My sense of touch that went beyond the physical felt it.*

About an hour later, I still could not vomit. I went to the bathroom. I could not see. I hesitated, turning on the light, for I did not want it to impede any visions that I could have had. *"Oh well,"* I said inside my head.

When I finally turned on the light, I saw that it shone differently. It was dimmer. I turned on the shower, and then went to get the water bin so that I could rinse it. I returned the water bin to my bed near the night table.

Inside the shower, I looked down at the floor. Figures of the same extraterrestrials appeared on the grey-white tiles with menacing countenances. I briefly considered urinating on them.

"No, go use the toilet."

After doing a number one and showering, I returned to bed. I looked straight ahead of me, at the desk and the computer that were across the opposite wall. The room looked and felt normal, as if I had not eaten the Peyote fruit.

A few minutes later, I looked at the window, to the left of the room. A few extraterrestrials—the same ones in Light body form appeared as in the last Peyote intake three months ago. Though I would have difficulty describing them physically now, if I saw them, I would definitely recognize them right away. Their slanted eyes at the brows stayed with me.

I lied flat in the bed with my eyes open, staring at them. I knew they were sneaky, and could not be trusted. However, they were about to reveal to me the extent of their malicious deviousness.

"Let him have his Emma love story," one of them said.

He was talking to one of his council members: one of his gang members.

"Every time we take someone from him, he just grabs onto it."

"What in the world are they talking about?"

Though my mind posed the question, at the fundamental level, I understood perfectly well what they were indeed saying. There were two possible answers. First, they were indirectly responsible for "those" they had taken away from me in each life incarnation; or second, because they felt they were the masters of the Third Dimension, they thought they could take ownership for my losses.

I maintained my eyes upon them, but did not speak. I brooded about how they could have been playing with events in my life. Such machinations and manipulations went beyond this life. I found it quite fascinating how these beings were able to do this. In their admission that "every time they took someone" from me, they were conceding that every opportunity they deprived me of love, my desire to know it grew. This was further proof that *love* or *a flicker* of light always wins despite its size. They know this, but yet are choosing to fight against the current of the river! This, in a way, is a lack of intelligence.

I offered the being speaking silence, but he soon disappeared. I turned my eyes to the bathroom door. Nothing! I scanned the entire room. Still nothing! Suddenly, I was seized by the throat again. I felt like vomiting, but nothing came. Just like the Ayahuasca session, my throat was dry—*water!* I looked around for something to drink.

No, I can't!

Besides, there wasn't any water in the room. I was also very hungry. If that was not enough, I felt a sexual sensation in my private part.

This is not the time for this.

I lied down with my head leaning down over the side of the bed, near the night table and the water bin to my left, ready to vomit if needed. I had a few close calls, but nothing really came. However, I coughed a lot, hoping to initiate a trigger that would expel some more entities.

As I coughed the being seized my left jaw, which I wriggled. I drew out long breaths. It moved about in my jaw.

No! It was not going to resist so easily. I need another strategy, but what?

I squeezed my stomach as I did during the Ayahuasca ceremony and coughed. My attempts were futile.

Though the coughs were unsuccessful, what transpire next brought me face to face with the true nature of what I was dealing with. A red demon appeared before me. It was humongous. It had a formidable body and super human strength. His vibrational energy made it clear to me that he was definitely either inter-dimensional or galactic. His very vibration radiated information that needed not be spoken. I understood that I was in a dimension above the third. The beast radiated fear and I understood that fear is a tool that is also employed in the fourth dimension. I clearly recall thinking: *Fear is used even here?* Though I could not physically perceive the extraterrestrials, I sensed their presence. I immediately understood that beings or souls that depart the third dimension have to go pass them in this dimension. I also understood immediately that this beast's raison d'être was to keep beings like me in line so as not to break the cycle of human slavery.

No! This entity in my body was not placed using any Black Magic that exists in this third dimension. These so-called extraterrestrials know my past better than my current conscious mind knows itself.

The beast said something about blocking my access to all gateways (i.e., dimensions), but I could not remember his exact words. I was more focused on the intuitive knowledge that was penetrating my mind. This demon beast was a super being. It looked as if it comprised several demons. The interesting thing about him was that he did not manifest nor did I sense a desire from him to hurt me.

Whatever he was saying, I wished I had paid more attention.

As I write now the demon-beast no longer seems beastly. In a way, he is my creation. I have shaped him. His desire for meat and sex came from my overindulgences: meat in this life and sex in previous lives. *He has a free-will of his own now.*

The super demon was gone from my third eye. I positioned myself in bed, ready to sleep, but I knew sleep would not come just yet. My eyes remained open. I looked toward the direction which the extraterrestrial had declared that they control everything. *Nothing!* I put the covers over myself, keeping my eyes open just in case. Then my "convergence" question was answered. It began with my soul showing me images of three light, fluid bodies. The first had much darkness. The last was the most clear. An intuitive message without words was communicated to me.

There are several ways of cleansing the body.

The last image was brought to the forefront. It was evident that this was the most efficient way to cleanse the body—at the soul or the Most Light body level. I agreed, but only had a hint of how to do this.

My focus went to the middle of the room. Something was happening toward the bathroom. A mixture of music-like sounds was playing, and would play throughout the majority of the rest of the experience.

The visual and images of what happened next is a little difficult to describe. The sound increased. A wave of intelligent energy filled the room. It was as if a being who was me but not was among them. Waves of different time periods fused into one—the past and future lives entered the room in waves of energy. They were one. Everything was happening simultaneously. I saw a few beings going in and out of time.

Really? How could my future infinite genius Me be among them?

I also sensed these super genius extraterrestrials. One thing was absolutely clear: my or their intelligence could only take them so far in their souls' journey. They were devoid of wisdom (i.e., spirituality). Though I did not know how the past, present, and future events could be happening at once, I understood that what transpired in the future has an effect on the past and perhaps both. My soul and the medicine already knew that I still was not convinced that I am from the future. Thus, every possible doubt that my mind could grab onto was put to the test. Every image and thoughts of doubts that I had while proctoring the midterms and the Regents exams in January of 2012 were casted away.

At times I found myself in the country in the United States, in Africa, and God knows where else. Finally, I was returned to the *new game*. I saw myself writing something, which two of the deceptive entities were watching intently. This was about the "Emma love story." A new game had indeed begun, which these extraterrestrials could observe and partake in. They would not be forced to engage in it. They knew this and smiled. I was aware that they thought they were still in control, and to a certain extent, they were. They were in control of their own actions, not mine. Besides, I suspected that they only admitted that they were in control because they knew I was now consciously aware of it. Recall that my soul had said that I would no longer get any interference from them.

Sunday, February 19, 2012:

I went to see don Mateo at 8:15 in the morning. He told me to put my hands forth. He observed them with interest. He then put Jesus Christ's cross in the right palm and closed the other hand over it. He then sucked around my back as well as my heart area. The vomiting then ensued on his part. When he was finished, he sat down across from me.

"You have a lot of luck here. A lot of luck. You have two crosses."

I looked at both of my hands. They do definitely have more than one cross.

The Double Cross

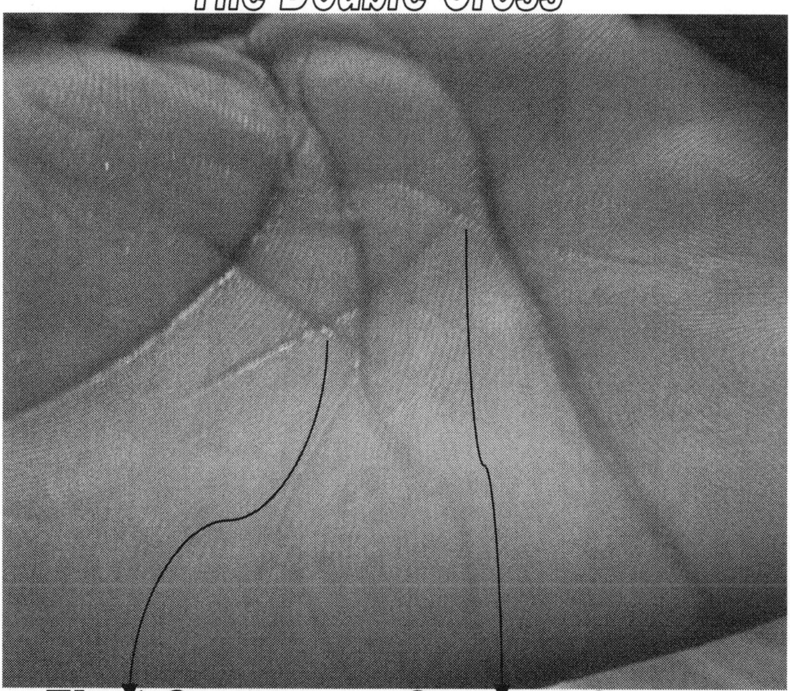

I briefly thought about the Christ consciousness. *No, this is more than luck. The "cross" is a symbol, not merely a*

religious symbol. Without knowing why, it intuitively dawned on me that this could be a huge sign about my true origins before I came to this planet.

Don Mateo stood up and turned his back to me as he prayed over something on his high table. About two minutes later, he faced me with a Peyote fruit, which he handed to me to eat.

"I had some last night," I said to him.

"I prayed over this one last night. When you chew, chew it very slowly so that you can commune with the spirit of the plant."

I did exactly as he instructed. He talked as I chewed slowly, with a bitter look on my face.

"You should not take any more Peyote tonight. You have to give it time for the experience to settle in. It's not good to take them back to back."

I did mention to him earlier that I intended to take some more in the evening. However, after considering his comments, I decided to take his advice.

"After all that I have done, the demon didn't want to come out."

"It's a part of you," he said, substantiating the belief system that the evil came from my own soul.

"No, it's definitely not a part of me. It's a galactic demon entity."

"Maybe you can use him to your advantage. Why not make friends with him?"

I had considered the thought in Peru, but I mostly did not know how.

"What about the plant bath?"

"You want to take a bath?"

I did not know why my request surprised him, for it was he who mentioned it during our last session nearly three months ago.

"The shadow is very deep. I have had Ayahuasca and Peyote healings, but none seemed to finish off the whole affair."

"You have to heal yourself now; to go beyond the material body into the spiritual," he said.

This matched part of the vision of self-healing that I had about a month before I came.

"But I don't know how to do that," I told him.

"I want you to *feel* today. No thinking. Focus on how you *feel*," he said as if nicely commanding me.

As I walked away I started thinking about how I would make friends with the inter-dimensional entity within me. I decided to start with what was near my heart. At 3:18 p.m., I put pen to paper not knowing exactly how to begin.

Dear Universe,

I am sorry for whatever I have done in the future. I am sorry for having joined this group of extraterrestrials and for helping to maintain this control system. I am sorry for anyone whom I may have harmed in the future more than 10,000 years ago. I was foolish to join the dark side. I now turn to you, the super demon being inside me who is refusing to come out. I understand now that there is something or things that link you to me at the mind level. Whatever I have done, I am no longer identifying with what impelled me to such actions. Release yourself of this pain as well. It is not necessary to carry all that load. Those entities with whom you are working want to keep you a slave. They do not want you to seek healing. They have manipulated you, and are definitely using you. If it is control you seek, you can have a lot more freedom when you let go. No matter how unbelievable this might seem to you now, there is still a force in you that will compel those using you to step aside. Their intelligence is futile, for they are negating love. Remember the Ayahuasca session when I saw these beings controlling the system? Recall that there was a force over them that was really making sure that things work out for the best. These beings came directly from God, and they will be here to aid you to escape from the system.

Believe you me, the system will fall with or without your acquiescence. Love is the ultimate power. Do you not remember that? Do you not remember what was said in the vision last night about it? Every time you guys have taken a loved one from me, I have held onto the lost. Do you not see that that is the precise reason for resisting your control system? From this day on I will no longer be playing your game of fear nor negotiating friendship with terrorists. I have played this game so long that I am honestly bored. Love now fascinates me. I derive more smiles and joy from it. I encourage you to think of a time when you were beautiful, a time when you felt unconditional love, a time when you felt no guilt. Infinity awaits you. Infinity must have you back. May the purest part of you talk to me about how to help you.

Several thoughts of doubts entered my mind as I wrote the letter. First, I recalled spending two weeks in the Amazon jungle trying to convince the entities that *love* is the best way, but they never listened. So, what made me think that they would listen this time?

Monday, February 20, 2012:

When I got out of bed that day, one thing was absolutely certain: Time traveling for me was a fact of universal life, and is being used today to go from dimension to dimension; within time and probably out of time.

It was now 1:30 p.m. My neck problem had persisted. I also felt palpitations in my left arm and both of my legs. I have had a bit of a hard time piecing together the information that I received last night. These entities were caught in the intellect, the mind. This was most interesting to me because these beings existed beyond physical form. They have existed for a very, very long time. They control planets and dimensions, but yet they are spiritually dead. Their strength is not strength at all.

Another interesting thing that I remarked is that any association with them is a creation of permanent hell. It is like being a member of the Mafia, but worse. Once you associate with them, it takes many, many life times to undo the death strangle choke-hold they have on you. Those souls out there in the U.F.O. community negating and swearing up and down that we face no threat from extraterrestrial foes are blind, foolish, and will be manipulated.

Tonight, I will eat the last batch of the Peyote plant. I really do not know what to expect in terms of healing. I thought the first session two days ago would have gotten rid of the demons in my neck.

I started chewing the remaining six Peyote fruit at 4:32 p.m. I chewed them very slowly. I finished at 5:05 p.m. I minced every piece as I did during don Mateo's session. I realized that I did not have to rinse my mouth with water or soda this time around. I felt movement in left the upper stomach area near my chest.

It is now 5:46 p.m. I finished showering and developed a strategy for tonight's session.

For the next three hours, I smoked some organic Peruvian tobacco, listened to Adele 21 songs as I stared into the water in the bucket. It usually takes about an hour and a half for the effect to kick in, but there I was three hours later. I suspected that something might be wrong. But then, the cold returned to my body. During this time, I paid heed to the message that I received about healing from the soul level and tried to open up my energy centers. I also called for the spirit of don Mescalito to help me vomit. I kept my mouth close to the water bin. I continued trying to open up my chakra center using my thoughts. I felt energy throughout my body. But, I was so cold—my feet especially. The bed had several heavy sheets. The heater was not on. I did not remember being this cold the last time I was here..

At about 11:50 p.m. I decided to take another shower. I did not really think the medicine was working since I did not feel any in my sight or vision. The shower did me good. I listened to Adele a little longer and went to bed. Again, I focused on opening up my energy centers to expel the beast. I felt a warm light penetrating the center of my head. I took this as my soul at work aiding me through the process. *Nothing!*

It must have been about 1 a.m. when I went to take a shower again. As the hot water sprinkled over my body, I began seeing reptiles: dragons, snakes, and frog-like creatures on the shower walls.

I turned and wiped my face with some water. Then, as if seized with a sudden epiphany, my hands would not leave my eyes. There it was in my left hand—*EYES!* I turned to my other hand. *EYES!* All of my fingers except the thumb had eyes.

I returned to my desk. Thoughts were flowing to me fast now. I've been trying to get rid of this being inside my body for a while.

What if it stayed just a little longer so that I can understand him.

I began to reexamine my strong urge to cast it way. I relaxed. I no longer had the need to cast it out so quickly. There will be plenty of time for that. I've grown this beast by feeding it low negative energy.

He needs a good teacher. But what am I feeding my ego? What's that anyway? How long will I allow the beast to stay within me now? I have another trip coming up soon—in a month and a half. This is not enough time to teach the beast to love.

Then I remembered the vision that I had where my body was totally clear of dark entities. Nausea welled up in my throat. I did not force it. If the beast wanted to stay, then that will give me time to understand him better: a chance to retrace my steps to learn the bigger purpose of why he is in my body.

I am not going to die being his teacher.

These were conflicting thoughts.

But haven't I been a good teacher nearly the last three years when I gave up eating meat? Isn't three years a long time? What about all the times when I refused to have sex for a "quick fix, a thrill?" If the beast has not learned to love a little, then when will he?

This was the best environment and situation for him to learn.

A good teacher?

A part of him was always asking for one. I am his teacher and my soul is my teacher. I did not listen at first.

No! This beast is not going to listen easily. It will have to suffer quite a bit to give up some of his negative ways. My mind is much lighter than his (i.e., cleaner) and if it took me a little over thirty years to give up meat, then what makes me think that the beast will accept love so easily? He won't!

My mind switched to the temperature in the room.

The cold serves a purpose? To keep me awake? Far out!

Seriously? I was writing fast now. Why wasn't it all clear to me a few hours ago? The Ensemble needs more teachers who can take crap. Disappointment, depression, loneliness, intellectual pride! These extraterrestrials feed off anything you give them.

I got into bed.

"You liked women a little too much…This time you chose wisely," the Togolese plant healer said with a smile.

So that is why I have not had many sexual partners in this life. In my previous incarnation I must have grown the beast tremendously with my sexual desires. The past, the present, and the future are all connected. I came here to stop myself. What I have done in the past incarnation stayed with me—a chance to become aware. Now, the beast is out of control. Three years to cast out the entity and he is still there?

Tuesday, February 21, 2012:

The time is now 3:23 a.m. I am still not asleep. I am trying to decide whether or not to stay awake or to fall asleep. Wow! The beast really exists. *The groin!* The beast wanted to be fed. *Don't identify with it—it's not my need.* The warm light within the center top of my head is getting stronger. "He'll just grab onto it!" replayed in my mind. The extraterrestrial being was right. I have been grabbing onto love. There were major souls in my life who I have lost that I could never forget: my childhood ram friend, my brother, my father, the dog that came to lick my face out of nowhere and insisted that I pet him when Harry was helping me to find a place to live, and many more.

What is love? The manifestations of love? This is what the extraterrestrials cannot fight against.

It is now about 4:15 a.m. I heard myself writing down: "*Must come back for Emma if necessary. When?*"

Yet, it was not an intent I was sure I would accomplish. There are thousands and thousands of girls in Mexico City. I only have two information to go on: her first name and the fact that she studied international relations or affairs.

This is insane! You snooze, you lose. Move on!

I woke up that morning uttering a firm statement, "The reptiles control this dimension and the next. David Icke was right. Their signs are everywhere. I picked up the big bottle of mineral water by my writing desk (i.e., seltzer water). The picture on the bottle depicted a woman or perhaps a man bowing down to drink some water. He is on his knees. To his right, above is a reptile that looks like a crocodile.

10:30 a.m.:

There was a time when I desperately wanted to go home. My body tormented me literally. Between 2002 and 2004 I wrote a novel about 450 pages, which I lost.

In time all thoughts are understood. I was writing about reincarnation and flying spirits, though I did not believe in such things. The main character kept saying over and over throughout the novel: "I want to go home."

Yet, he had no idea where home was. I thought about my earthly native land in West Africa. I like my language and culture, but when I returned in 2000, I did not feel like this was my ultimate home. I have asked myself over and over again in America if the various cultures I have been a part of accurately described me. No! They did not.

In the novel Eweland, I focused on what society expected me to say whenever people asked me where I from. Often I told them Togo. They usually asked where that was and I would explain. It usually seemed to me that we were dwelling on this too much, for by asking all those questions about Africa and America, the person posing the questions still had not gotten anywhere close to knowing who I am. It was usually as if we were creating a distorted perception of who we human beings really are. It seemed like a vicious cycle that kept us in a limited static perception of the Universe. Ever since I was in France in 1999, I wanted to say what I really felt, but I felt powerless to perform this magnificent task. As I sat by the municipal office by the ATM machine in Real de Catorce, I knew things were different this time.

A man came up to me posing a question that I had heard at least a dozen times since I arrived.

"Where are you from?"

"I am from your heart, where religion doesn't exist, where our fake science does not exist, where there is only the stillness of unconditional love."

He looked at me with confusion.

"What are you writing?"

"A book about who we are."

Another man comes out of a store.

"That's good, to write a book."

"Yeah," I said, enjoying the sun. I was wearing my black rain jacket. They left me.

Wednesday, February 22, 2012:

After getting off the bus in DF, I returned to the place where I had once met Emma. The bus arrived about an hour early. I waited there until 7:30, somehow knowing that it would be to no avail; nevertheless, I waited. I left, disappointed at myself and remained in this state of mind all day. I stopped near the entrance—about 8 or ten minutes away from the airport. There were young women selling breakfast. I stopped to eat.

It took me about eleven or twelve minutes to get to the baggage check-in. However, as soon as I handed the passport to the young man, I realized that I had left my bag that contained the paintings for the cover of this very book. Some of the paintings were dead on and there was no way I was going to leave Mexico without them.

I ran back. I must have looked at the time on my cell phone at least half a dozen times. When I arrived, the young lady by whom I had left the bag smiled and handed it to me. I took it and started running toward the airport again. I stopped to look at the time on my cell phone. Then, I turned to take a taxi, for I knew that there was no way I was going to make it on time even if I ran. To make a long story short, I made it to the plane on time.

Going from Mexico City to Texas was of no incident. However, I cannot say the same for my connecting flight to LaGuardia Airport. As it has happened before during the last couple of months, I was asked to go into a full-body scanner section. And as always, I refused. A tall black man patted my body down. Unlike the others who did this in the previous months, this one was polite and nice, but was convinced that I was exaggerating vis-à-vis the stand I was making.

"I have a friend who will not drink milk. She swears that our food is poisonous."

"You're friend is right. All of our food is poisoned. What's happening with this scanner is just a little piece of the battle," I said.

"The scanner only has a very small amount of radiation."

"Yeah? I'd like to see people put their babies through them."

"You use a cell phone," he said confidently.

"I use ear phones and the loud speakers."

"You don't."

"Yes I do," I said adamantly.

It is true that it has only been about two and a half months since I have started.

"I think I know where you are going with this," he said, moving forward toward his colleague, "Unless you're going to change the overall system, then nothing is going to change."

At this point, an older black man came out of an office to my left.

"What's going on here?" he asked like a man in charge.

I observed him with questioning eyes.

"He's alright. We're just having a conversation," the nice black man said.

What was perplexing about this whole experience was that people just went through the scanners like lambs just because they were told to do so by "authority" without questions.

I made it to the plane on time. I began thinking about the concept of denial, which I define as the refusal to accept or believe that which is true despite fully knowing that it is indeed so. Denial comes in many forms and in many disguises. Sometimes the reason why we deny is quite clear. At other times, the reason is not so evident. Denial hides in the recess of our minds. Thus, a part of the unconscious self is always aware of it even though the everyday unconscious self is not.

Sometimes we use the denial to inflict pain on ourselves—to self-punish. All of this hinders us from finding lasting healing. As I sat in the plane, I began to think about karma and forgiveness. One of the things that entered my mind was one of Dr. Brian Weiss's books. Later when I would return to the States, I would open up the book where he indirectly spoke about this in terms of free will and destiny. This was done through one of the main characters called John.

When he first met him, John announced that he was a wealthy man. Dr. Weiss states that John's small ironies covered large wounds. John grew up overly cloistered. He was like a tapestry on his parents' walls, beautiful and finely crafted, but nothing more than an adornment. He had one abiding interest: women, the female form. He had one-night stands, fleeting dalliances. Even when he married, he felt nothing profound. The marriage was more of a business arrangement. Dr. Weiss's questions were met with an airy dismissal of any ambition and goals in his life. It was only when the doctor decided to provoke him did the veneer crack.

"Lately, I haven't been able to sleep. Never on my own, and there isn't a drug powerful enough to keep me under for more than an hour or two."

"What force is so powerful that it doesn't let you sleep?" the doctor asked.

John struggled to keep his voice calm—and failed.

"Terror, Dr. Weiss. Unremitting, abject terror."

When I read these words years before, they had very little effect on me. However, after my Ayahuasca experience, something pushed me to go back to John's story as I mentioned before. Like John, I too could not sleep. No drug was powerful enough to allow me to "fall" and stay asleep for more than a few hours. This was definitely an improvement compared to the pre-Ayahuasca experience.

I returned my mind to John's story.

"Terror of what?" Dr. Weiss asked with the hair on his arms rising.

"Of death. I run and run and run from the fear, but it always catches up. The women—they're just a diversion. So was any job I ever took. Nothing drove away the fear…I won't drive, can't drive. Our house has more alarm systems than a Mafia don's…A sudden loud noise? I'm under the table. I'm a Vietnam vet with PTSD [Post Traumatic Stress Disorder], only I've never been to war…Last week I heard a car backfire, and I fainted, passed out."

This time around, I took John's words seriously, and given that the book was about past lives, I knew that his sleep problem had its roots in a previous life. Dr. Weiss put him under hypnosis where John found himself a great warrior, a warrior-king. He and his men committed atrocities such as raping other men's wives and daughters, roasting babies on spits, setting fires to cities. When Dr. Weiss brought him back from the hypnosis, John was staggered by the extent of his cruelty, horrified that in whatever life, in whatever persona, he was capable of rape and murder.

I too committed horrific crimes like John that would not let me sleep.

Dr. Weiss comforted him by telling him that he suspected that he paid for it, and took him to another past incarnation in England. It was during the time of the Great Fire. He found himself in a drunken sleep from which he could not awake. His daughter was with him.

"I could hear Alice screaming as her hair caught fire, but the screams soon stopped. I supposed that, mercifully, she had died. Death came for me, too, but it took its time. The flames seemed to crawl their way up my body rather than taking me whole. My legs burned first, then my torso, and only after a long time my head. It was as though I was being crucified for sins like drunkenness and adultery—bad sins, I admit, but I didn't seem to deserve such a cruel sentence of death."

When I first read his story years ago, I smiled and even laughed a little thinking: *He deserved it.* But, I am not laughing now, for I found myself in the same predicament. The fact that centuries passed before he would be severely "punished" and for him to be able to empathize with his victims peaked my interest.

I recalled telling my shaman don Herberto that my problems did not began in this consciousness.

"*I am not innocent,*" I heard my mind say, but a part of me quickly sought to offset this.

"*How do you really know? What evidence do you have for this. You can't just believe it. Remember, believing got you into trouble before.*"

Then another part of my mind fought back.

"Ayahuasca is a powerful medicine." It took three sessions to begin vomiting. Isn't this curious to you?"

My innocence was lost. I no longer view Barack Obama, the Pope, Hilary Clinton, and the likes as evil, but rather as foolish and naïve to that which awaits them if they do not cease their wicked ways. I am now like the main character Raskonikov in Dostoïevski's novel Crime and Punishment, which I read in French in France in 1999. I had committed horrible crimes and only now was headed toward redemption.

How can I ever see criminals, murders, and wrongdoers differently from myself now? My innocence is lost. I was never innocent.

In 2009 when I became aware that Black Magic was casted on me, I actually told my mother, "We cannot do any harm." It was my supposed innocence that carried me through. I thought I was on higher ground because I "had not provoked" any of the pain and torture inflicted on me.

I remained immobile for the longest time in my seat on the airplane, starring at the void in front of me. I was in a daze, a stupor.

I twisted my neck to relieve the discomfort brought by the demon-beast. A part of me wanted to just sleep while another part compelled me to transcribe the notes that I had written on small pieces of paper and napkins into this yellow-grey journal in which I am currently writing. As I copied and added to the notes that I had written, I was overcome with a sense of guilt. It all became clear to me and I could no longer deny that which my soul had been telling me. I was crying as I wrote.

"How could I have been on the dark side? What have I done?"

So, this was the real reason why the demon-beast refused to come out of my body. I was stopping it through guilt of what I have done. I was punishing myself quotidianly without consciously being aware of it. I mean, who eats twelve Peyote fruit and does not vomit and or take a crap? It made no sense. No wonder I suffered so much. *I caused it! To undo the harm that I had done thousands of years in the future, I had accepted to suffer.* It dawned on me that my crimes are really, really huge: *at the galactic level?* I mean, I was part of those who either assisted or were directly controlling this planet and beyond. I stopped writing to stare at the void in front of me. I understood now why I did not take Emma's contact information. It was not because I did not want to be in love. It was because I did not think I deserved it. I was still punishing myself for whatever I had done.

But how do I forgive myself?

I turned left to look at the woman sitting to the left of me.

She too definitely has skeletons in her closest. Everyone has something alive inside. She has just finished eating a genetically modified meat sandwich of some sort. She's definitely feeding her beast.

For a long time, I have fed my beast through negativity and pretended that I was not the cause of my own suffering. Now, it is absolutely clear to me that I indeed knew that there was something wrong, very, very wrong. I could not pin point it at the time, and did nothing thinking and hoping that with time it would go away. That's insanity! There I was literally being f—ed deep in the ass by an unknown force in 2005 and kept thinking that it would go away by itself. *How insane!* I mean, *how far up the hole did this demon's cock have to enter before I said no?*

I did not stop the demon because I ignored my own intuition. This is precisely what human beings are doing right now. Evil demonic entities such as the Bush family, Sarkozy, and Obama are screwing you hard in the ass and people are ignoring it. How far up our ass does the d--k have to be before we know we are being f—ed? Must you know exactly who's screwing you to admit that something is terribly wrong? How deep must the penetration be before you know there is a violation? How much must it hurt? How much must you cry within your own skin? Humanity is insane. I was insane!

I turned back to the seat in front of me.

How do I forgive myself? Emma!

That was my soul trying to help me to forgive myself. Love, unconditional love transcends all barriers, that was what my soul was trying to tell me during the first Peyote session. My mind was refusing to move on. As I write now, I do not know what the future holds, but this struggle is harder than I could ever imagine. I once said that the biggest battle is within the self, and now I was experiencing it personally.

I wanted to understand why Emma was put in front of me so as to understand love, not necessarily to be with her, but to understand. I was not sure I was ready for unconditional love, but yet a part of me pushed me on to keep debating the issue in my head.

I can't regress.

Yet, all I wanted to do was to live in isolation, away from civilization, to be an island without contact to other souls. Yet, I knew this was not the best path to take.

As I sat in the plane, a part of me wanted to throw away the book I was writing—*another form of self-punishment*.

Saturday, February 25, 2012:

The time was 1:09 p.m. I have been writing and crying since I got up this morning. I still did not know what it is that I did more than 10,000 years in the future that has contributed to the current slave state of humanity. But whatever it is, it was terribly fantastic.

On Thursday morning, two days ago, a spider web seized my face as I passed room 162 in the middle of hallway at the high school where I teach. I did not believe that it was a real spider web.

In the middle of the hallway?

I went to the foreign language office to print some documents for my morning classes. A few minutes later, the spider web disappeared without me touching my face. That was when I knew that it was an inter-dimensional entity contact. As I mentioned before, this has been happening for the last three years. This latter web was particularly strong.

The time was now 1:18 p.m. *It's time to stop punishing myself.*

"But how do I do this?"

I did not know, but I am NOT descending. What if I could put all my strength in the positive NOW. What if? *It's done! To the Light! The luminosity of the purity of the light. Let go! Move on!*

The time was now 8:53 p.m. I must have cried five or six different times today. It was only after shedding the tears that I was able to feel slightly better. I have spent the vast majority of my day thinking about whether or not I have suffered enough to move on, to release the demon-beast within. I thought about all the time that I was majorly despondent and depressed, about the late summer of 2007. I also remembered endless nights in 2005 when I could not sleep because of general bodily torture. I wanted to analyze the dilemma to come to my own conclusion. First, I have suffered a lot in this life. Second, events were coordinated for me to meet a girl to help me with love. And thirdly, I did receive a message that my body will be cleared. If that is the case, then the logical answer is that I have paid enough of my dues to be released. The rest of the payment will be paid in kindness by writing and sharing information with people.

At about 10 p.m. I went on Google.com to learn more about the demon-beast. Google directed me to Revelation 11:7, 13:1-10 and 17:7-18. I started with 11:7, which read:

> *And when they have finished their testimony, the beast that ascends from the bottomless pit will make war upon them and conquer them and kill them.*

That was not what I was looking for. I was hoping to find a detailed description of the demon-beast as I had experienced it. I turned to 13:1-10:

> *And I saw a beast rising out of the sea, with ten horns and seven heads, with ten diadems upon its horns and a blasphemous name upon its heads. And the beast that I saw was like a leopard, its feet were like a bear's, and its mouth was like a lion*

> *mouth...Men worshipped the dragon for he had given his authority to the beast...*

This was a little better, but the descriptions were still not akin to mine. There were also no mention about the fact that the demon-beast exists in our physical bodies. I took the word "worship" as giving into incessant urges, desires. We accept such desires as emanating from our true self, and not a different force within us. As such, we worship the beast. Revelation 17:7-18 doesn't tell us much, so will not be described here.

After reading Revelations, I made a mental note:

The truth is presented in bits and pieces in religions and our mostly-false science.

A few days before returning to Mexico, I received a letter from the Teachers Association which read:

> In reference to the above-captioned grievance which the Association filed on your behalf, please be advised that we have reached an agreement with the District. During the 2012-2013 school year, you will be assigned three (3) preps and no duty period.
>
> If you have any questions, please do not hesitate to contact me.
>
> Very truly yours,
>
> George...

The letter was dated February 2012 and contained the Association's name with its address, e-mail, website, fax and phone number.

I responded with the following letter:

> Hello Mr. S and M.G.,
>
> Sorry for not answering right away to the February 9, 2012 letter that I received on the 15th. I was away for a few days. The grievance (RE: Epou, et al. Grievance) letter that I received reads…

The following was my response on February 28, 2012 at 7:08 p.m.

> I have three concerns with this decision. First, I still have a duty period as of now, 2-28-2012 with four (4) preps, which I should not have given the current breach in the contract. Second, the decision does not address or solve the problem—that the contract has been violated every year since I have been there. Thirdly, if I am split between the two buildings next year, I would not have a duty period anyway, so this is not a rectification of the overload in the teaching preparations that I have had since I have started working at the District.
>
> I strongly believe that the decision is not just and should proceed to arbitration. If there is no intention for this to be carried out, then I would appreciate being informed.

Agbe

Friday, March 2, 2012:

I was in the parking lot of my apartment complex. I had just returned from work. I was in the driver's seat with my head hung down. The super demon weighed heavily upon my upper shoulders and neck. I wanted immediate relief. I became irritated.

"What's wrong with you?" I said very loudly inside my head.

I twisted my neck, trying to crack it as usual.

"You're an asshole. You like suffering. Release me! Everyone else has left it go. Your ultimate self has said it's time to move on. Tell me I was not brutally killed in previous lives! Didn't an army of demons possess my body for 17 years?! What else do you want from me?"

Reader, as you may have guessed, I was talking to that part of me that had unconscious knowledge about my past lives beyond this life time. This was the same part of me that refused love in Mexico recently.

My conscious self considered punishing this unconscious part of me. I wanted to give him an ultimatum, but I knew it was all futile. He probably would have liked it if I punished him some more. I was at a dead-end and had to endure the suffering until at least April.

"Only one force is capable of crossing all barriers," I reminded myself. Thus, I stopped the monologue inside my head. I decided that the best

thing to do now was to go forward, to find once again a quiet place within the turmoil, to reside in the center, maintaining the calmness of tranquility until I could be freed. Millennia have passed where I shook within the center of chaos. Now my waking consciousness was resolute. *I will not falter. Love engenders love. I long for peace despite my mind. Love is categorically not only possible but real.*

CHAPTER 13

FINALLY ESCAPING FROM THE THIRD DIMENSION

When I started writing this book, I asked myself how I would know when I have escaped from the Third Dimension. It was only after I returned to the United States from my Ayahuasca trip that I finally accomplished this huge task. I was at a Costco gas station in upstate New York, and it was late in the afternoon. I was waiting for my turn to pump gas at the second to the left lane when suddenly, I became emotional.

"Will Mother Earth remember that I was once on this planet? I'll miss you."

I was in a state of deep wonder. My mind was outside this dimension as I thought about another world—a beautiful consciousness I could vaguely remember.

I was feeling a bit nostalgic. *I am here now, and this is the planet* (i.e., Earth) which I have inhabited for at least a few millennia and only now I feel strong enough to escape its confinement. Yet, as I sat there in the driver's seat in my car, I knew I had already escaped from the Third Dimension. When you desperately want to escape your fears, you must stay—to turn and wheel around the sword of truth and courage. When you no longer want to leave, then it is time to leave—but only when the job is done. And the job is not done yet.

This is my home now. *Deep, simple!* Love baffles—it compels and renders us to our knees, metaphorically; and finally when the time is right, it drives us to action and we are willing to give up all that we have planned since time immemorial. Each incarnation had prepared me to be at this precipice of change and I have NO INTENTION of waiting for another ten thousand years to see the consciousness of this Earth rise.

Tuesday, April 10, 2012:

I feel like a little boy walking around with a delicious secret. I am in Costa Rica now. I have been bed-ridden for three days because of the Iboga medicine. It worked so wonderfully that I do not even know where to begin.

To say that humanity has been manipulated through culture, religion, technology, and science is an understatement. Even now as I write, I feel like screaming out with pure exhilaration: *Yeah! Infinity, what else do you have?* Reader, remember that this book is a recipe for escaping from not only this Third Dimension but from all dimensions. In a way, it is a recipe to return home, to go to heaven.

Let us discuss two of my Iboga visions to underscore the beauty that awaits us if we should dare challenge this system for the better.

The first vision was the most delicious and happy-tear inspiring. I found myself in space. Right in front of me was a huge pier-like column of light going straight up. I understood that I was between the threshold of the third and fourth dimensions. I looked straight up and the blue-greenish light ascended into Infinity. I was free to go up the dimensions as I wished. I immediately became aware of a fantastic truth: If I should decide, this is the last time I will reincarnate in human form. Then, I recalled that I already had a brief vision of this about two weeks before coming to Costa Rica. I rushed up to the top, the very top: straight to the Source (i.e., God). Yet, I did not go home. "*Where's my brother?*" I heard myself saying. I descended again to what appeared to be the second dimension. I did not see him, and I became a little worried. I focused my third eye, and there he was on my right. He was along side of me. At that moment, I understood that I was around the seventh dimension. I was not even halfway through the dimensions even at this level. As my brother and I ascended, the colors became lighter, and I finally understood where I came from before this planet: Straight from God.

The next vision rendered my heart not only at peace, but also gave me further insight into the nature of each being in this and all local universes. I found myself in a room. I was in physical form. Straight ahead of me was a wall of flowing water. Somehow I understood that this intelligent being of water was an unconscious part of me.

"The Universe is expanding," he said.

"How can the Universe go on forever? How can it be limitless? I don't understand."

The intelligent water being looked at me for a moment, trying to find the best way to help me to understand. A picture of a void at the end of the Universe appeared before me. All in front of me was literally nothingness: no life, just a vast empty whole of nothingness.

"Out of this nothingness and emptiness, the Universe expands. Each being that advances creates new life."

Far out! I understood the message immediately. Each soul that advances has the will to eventually create his or her own local universe, thus expanding the total Universe. This was a lot more than I expected. The intelligent water being was not talking about each soul becoming a planet or a star; he was talking about AN ENTIRE *FREAKEN* UNIVERSE. *This is why we are struggling? How fantastic! Each of us can really become Gods in our own universes if we work at it. Too cool! So, the Universe expanding is a good thing.*

Reader, whatever obstacles you face, endure it. Do not give your power or sovereignty to culture, religion, race, and worse yet science. Do not let trivial pleasures such as sex, power, and money hold you back. Take no short-cuts, do not end your life prematurely. Genuinely smile as often as you can. And, if by chance you are caught between being killed and killing someone else, do not kill. What awaits the perpetrator is far worse than you can ever imagine. Watch what you eat and consume. The Universe is your playground. Play nicely with your fellow soul mates. I wish you luck because you are my soul mate. You are infinitely beautiful despite what you have done. We are all connected. Not even a static perception or illusion can separate us. Wake up my star people. You are the cavalry! REMEMBER WHO YOU ARE! Wake up Earthlings!

I think it is only appropriate that I end here with a poem that I wrote for Mother Earth.

> Will you recognize me beyond the physical? Beyond all ephemeral things such as culture, religion, and especially our mostly fake and false science?

I don't know how or exactly why, but I cry for you now because after thousands of years, my departure is now imminent. I feel a duality inside me. A part of me wants to stay here with you Mother Earth and Mother Ayahuasca, but a part of me also want to return to the bliss I once knew—so, so peaceful and calm—beyond imagination. The mind is astounded because of its static perception brought on by conditioning, by the dark ones and ourselves.

Thank you for the opportunity to have experienced on this planet. Mother Earth, thank you for your lack of rules, for those of us who do not need them. Thank you for that day when you gave me access to move around the entire planet simultaneously without restriction.

God speed everyone!

Printed in Great Britain
by Amazon

74959419R20179